Copyright 2024 © by D(
All Rights rese:
No part of this book m
reproduced in any manner whatsoever
including audio recording or AI without written permission of the author and Copyright holder. This author supports the right to free expression and values copyright protection.
The scanning, uploading, and distribution of
this book in any manner or medium without permission of the copyright holder is theft of the property. Thank you for supporting this author's
creative work with your purchase.
FIRST EDITION
Digital ISBN: 9798990323216
Paperback ISBN: 9798990323223
Editor: Lynne Pearson, All that Editing
This is a work of fiction. Names, characters, places, and incidents either are the product of the author's imagination or are used fictitiously, and any resemblance to actual persons, living or dead, business establishments, organizations, events, or locale, is entirely coincidental.

DEDICATION

To Judy, for all your love and support
over the last twenty-five years.
I am looking forward to more
road-trips over the next twenty-five.

CHAPTER ONE

That cute guy was crooking his finger. *Is he looking at me?* Tulsi Anthony glanced around at the thinning crowd. There was no one else except Cortland in the immediate vicinity. *Couldn't be for me.* "I think I need another Sea Breeze," Tulsi muttered to Cortland.

She chewed on the end of her swizzle stick. Her mood was low. She had hoped to make this move to Colby the start of a better life. A chance to build friendships and become an accepted part of the community. Even though she'd only been in town a week, her hopes were sinking already. Despite being at a table for half the clinic staff, she and Cortland were left behind when the office staff and vet techs decided to split for a party elsewhere. Tulsi sighed. *Abandoned yet again.*

One of her two best friends, Doctor Cortland Stewart, veterinarian extraordinaire, sat across the deserted table from her. Cortland wasn't drunk. She kept scanning the wedding reception crowd every few minutes. Her former boyfriend, Dawson, was somewhere in the event hall. Or had he left? Hannah and Andrew's wedding party was winding down, and few guests were remaining.

Oh no. Ugh, here we go. Hannah's mother was heading her way, walking a wobbly line. When a splash of liquid came out of her drink glass, Mrs. Woodbridge didn't notice.

"Dr. Anthony, I was hoping you would be wearing a sari tonight." The woman plopped down in the empty seat beside her. "I just love the colors. Indian women's attire is always so colorful. And it looks so comfortable." Mrs. Woodbridge slurred her words before taking another gulp of the amber liquid.

Tulsi smoothed her hands over the dove-gray satin gown. "Your daughter asked me to be a bridesmaid. So, I had to wear the dress she picked out for Cortland and me." It was a true statement. Far better than admitting she didn't own a sari. *Why do people always think that just because I'm of Indian ancestry, I would have a sari and know how to cook curries, eat dosa or naan, and practice yoga every day? At least she didn't ask me to do a Bollywood dance.*

Mrs. Woodbridge stood. "That's too bad. I'm sure you would have looked beautiful in one." She tottered away, heading in the direction of the bar so disjointedly Tulsi hoped the bartender would cut her off, and Mr. Woodbridge was driving that night.

Heaving a sigh, she eyed her watch. It was nearly midnight, and hopefully the festivities would end soon. Between the BFF bachelorette party last night and the wedding ceremony and reception today, she was exhausted. That didn't include her drive up from Louisiana a little over a week ago. Plus, moving into Cortland's former condo, settling in at the vet clinic, and, oh yeah, four days of work. Talk about being thrown into the fire.

She shook it off, sipping on the swizzle stick like it was a straw. Which it wasn't. She was grateful to have made it to Hannah and Andrew's wedding and honored to have been asked to serve as a bridesmaid. She scanned the hall. That slim, light brown-haired guy smiled when she met his gaze, and crooked his index finger again. *Wasn't he one of the groomsmen?* They hadn't formally met since there wasn't a rehearsal the night before. Unsure of his identity, she decided to ignore him.

He was mighty cute, as in baby-faced cute. A lock of hair flopped impudently onto his forehead. The rest of his hair was cut close to his scalp up the sides, without any barber-cut designs so popular these days. He beckoned with his index finger again. Tulsi figured he was signaling someone else. He couldn't be trying to entice her, could he?

Nearly everyone left in the hall had broken into couples except for her and Cortland. Her vision got a little fuzzy as her eyelids started to droop. And that was when, over Cortland's shoulder, she saw him advancing toward her. His index finger pointed straight at her, he mouthed "You," then gestured as if summoning her to come to him.

TULSI'S FLAME

Heat flushed through her face. His head bobbed toward the bar, and he used his crooked finger to lure her over to him.

Well, well. Maybe it is me he's gesturing toward. A twinge of sexual attraction made a smile blossom on her face. She lowered her eyes in a flirtatious manner, not yet willing to give in to his "come hither" gestures.

Cortland must have seen the expression on her face. She turned around and caught sight of him. "I think Lucas wants to dance with you." She leaned forward and whispered in Tulsi's ear, "Go get 'em, cowgirl," and gave her a wink.

Well now, his name was Lucas. *Should I go to him?* A twinge in her belly made up her mind. It had been a long time since her last sexual encounter, and this guy, Lucas, looked mighty fine. Slim but filled out muscularity with a sort of an inverted triangular face with big, round, brown eyes. Those baby face looks belied his age, which had to be at least equal to her own twenty-eight years. His dress pants hugged the curve of his ass and the thickness of his thighs. His chest, minus the suit jacket, was partially covered by a brilliant white dress shirt roguishly unbuttoned to mid-abdomen, giving a hint of tight abs.

Cortland's ear-to-ear grin and nod in his direction made up Tulsi's mind. Maybe it was time to get lucky tonight. She gulped down the last of her drink. "I'm going for another. Do you want anything?"

Cortland shook her head, and Tulsi set down the empty glass and stood. He had been part of the wedding party as a groomsman along with Dawson, she decided. Locking eyes with him, she tilted her head toward the bar. Lucas grinned and hastened to intercept her.

"Having a good time tonight?" he asked as he handed his empty beer bottle to the bartender. "Another, please. And anything this beauty wants."

"Sea Breeze." Tulsi flicked her bob-styled dark brown hair away from her eyes. "Yes, it's been fun. And great to see my girlfriends again. I've missed them."

His nod brought that loose lock of hair flopping down onto his forehead. He let it sit there, not bothering to brush it back. Did he have any idea how sexy that was? "You're the new veterinarian at the Colby Clinic, right?" he asked.

She smiled, her belly getting warmer, her heart beating faster. He was definitely revving her engine. "That's me. I'm replacing Cortland."

"I heard you three were tight in college."

"Vet school, yeah. It feels good to be back in New England."

A quizzical expression erupted on his face. "Where were you?"

"Small community in rural Louisiana. And glad to be out, let me tell you."

"That bad?"

"The stories I could tell." She held up her palm as if swearing on a Bible. "Every one of them true."

The bartender slid their fresh beverages across the countertop. He nodded his appreciation as

Lucas dropped a twenty-dollar bill in the tip jar.

They walked over to a cocktail table. Standing beside it, Tulsi sipped at the drink. This was her fourth Sea Breeze and she'd had two glasses of wine during dinner. She hadn't anticipated finding a man, so she hadn't held herself in check. Like Cortland, she would call an Uber to get home tonight. It hadn't been feasible to drive since the limo had picked them up with Hannah, the bride, and delivered them to the hall after the ceremony.

She eyed Lucas over her drink. He was definitely handsome. His body might be filled out like a man, but that baby face made him look like he should still be in high school. Something in it also gave Tulsi the impression he was not quite 100 percent Anglo-Saxon white male. Perhaps it was the darkness of his eyes, nearly black. And his skin looked tanned, like permanently tanned. *If I play my cards right, I can get him naked and find out if it's his natural skin tone or a tan.* She smiled rather than sip at her tiny cocktail.

"What's so funny?" he asked, leaning into her ear. His breath tickled her lobe, making her lady parts stir to attention even more.

The dancing was getting a little rowdy. There wasn't much time left before the venue closed for the night. Tulsi wondered if he was going to ask her to go home with him. *Scratch that. It's the twenty-first century. I'll ask him.* "I was thinking about going home—" she paused before adding, "with you."

His eyebrows shot up, making Lucas's eyes widen and glisten with amusement. "We'll have to go to your place. Tell me more." He raised his beer bottle to his lips and let the tip of his tongue taste the opening. "What do you think would happen?" He put the opening against his lips and sipped.

Tulsi's crotch flooded with wetness as her girl parts squeezed with anticipation. She raised an eyebrow in a way she hoped was flirtatious. "I think we would end up in my bed."

His hand ran the length of his beer bottle, shifting Tulsi's focus. "To sleep?"

Tulsi smiled over her drink again with a sparkle in her eyes. He was sexually flirting with her, and it was working big time. She slowly shook her head.

A growing smile filled his face, his eyes twinkling. Lucas swigged his beer.

She gnawed on her fresh swizzle stick. *Playing a cougar is kind of fun.* "That is, if you want to come home with me. In an Uber, of course."

The DJ interrupted to announce a song "requested by Hannah for C and D."

They both turned toward the dance floor. Lucas took her hand and jerked his head toward it. "Let's dance."

She hadn't been paying attention to the music or dancers during their conversation. As they advanced to the dance floor, she spied Cortland and Dawson. *Well now. That's good, isn't it?*

Lucas drew her attention back as he pulled her against his body, his dark brown soulful eyes searching hers. He swayed in place, taking her with him. Her focus shifted as she caught sight of Cortland stomping off the floor, leaving Dawson standing alone. Instinct pulled her to go after Cortland. But Lucas squeezed her tighter. When she shifted her attention back to him, she blurted the first thing she could think of. "How's Dawson feeling?" She jerked her head toward Dawson leaving the dance floor toward the exit, a slight limp in his gait.

"He's kind of messed up." His confession shocked her. That was not what she'd expected. Lucas swiftly continued, "His ankle is healing fine, but his heart...not so much."

"She's bummed he's not going to Alaska with her."

"He's really pissed she's leaving." Lucas pulled her closer. So close she could feel his erection pressed against her pubic bone. "Let's not talk about them," he whispered.

Growing dampness between her legs made Tulsi forget Cortland's predicament. She nodded and let her guard down, pushing her pelvis into his hard, muscular frame. His hand at her waist slid down to cup her buttocks. Instinctively, she rested her chin on his shoulder, letting his body's smooth movements spark more tension in her belly. Her chest widened with a deep breath as her arms tightened around his waist. She pulled him closer, crushing her torso against his so their bodies moved as one. Could he feel her erect nipples against his chest? She sure could feel the aching of her clit for his hardened cock.

The slow music faded in moments and a lively dance with a Latin beat thudded through the banquet hall.

Lucas stepped back and started doing a salsa, still holding one of her hands in his. He led her around the dance floor, cutting it up like he was some champion salsa dancer. Tulsi tried to follow what he was doing and let him twirl her. Based on his expertise, she would have to guess he had some Latino blood. Not that she cared. She had a dark skin tone, too, darker than his, in fact. She couldn't throw stones. There were much better things she had in mind to do to Lucas.

They zoomed and shimmied around the other dancers so actively that most couples stepped aside to watch them and clap to the music. His face, that body. Yikes, she nearly lost it watching him gyrate to the Latin music. The swelling and aching between her legs grew to new heights. He danced like one of those professionals on *Dancing with the Stars*...all confidence and bravado.

Toward the end of the song, Lucas told her. "I'm going to dip you at the end. Stay loose and trust me. I'll make sure you don't fall."

Tulsi couldn't believe it. She'd never been dipped before in her life. Then again, she never danced salsa, either. The music heightened as did her apprehension. This could go very badly, but the way Lucas moved so expertly to the music gave her reason to trust he wouldn't drop her.

When he called out, "Now," Tulsi let him dip her backward over his knee as if they had practiced it a million times. The watching crowd went wild with clapping and cheering. Pulling her upright, Lucas stepped to the side while holding her hand and bowed. Seeing it, Tulsi did her best impression of a curtsy. The small crowd roared again. As the applause died, the DJ thanked the dancers and wished them all safe travels wherever they were going next.

People were slow to leave, settling themselves in clusters around the hall. Tulsi looked for Cortland but didn't see her. Her gaze roamed for Dawson and found him resting his elbow on the bar, his head leaning into his open palm. *Drats! I was hoping they'd settle their differences and get back to being a couple again.*

"Where are you heading?" Lucas asked, a warm expression on his face.

"I'm thinking home is the only answer. Would you like to join me? The place is a mess with boxes everywhere. I haven't had time to unpack much of anything, but the bed is...ready."

"Sounds very tempting." Lucas's eyes darkened. "Did you like that last dance?"

"Yes. Where'd you learn to dance like that?"

Lucas chuckled, "I have two older sisters who enlisted me when they wanted to practice their dance moves. I caught on quick." When she nodded, he added, "Would you like to go to El Fuego for more dancing?"

Tulsi looked at him. Was El Fuego a bar or dance club? Besides her condo, the clinic, and the grocery store, she had no clue what the town held for fun. Hope shone brightly on Lucas's face as he waited for her answer, a promise of a delightful morning unspoken there. Watching this guy dance fired up her lady parts. Building a little more sexual tension sounded like an interesting idea. "Let's do it."

CHAPTER TWO

Tulsi heard the music spilling out of El Fuego from a block away. The cab dropped them off at the front door to the club, set in a three-story brick building in an older section of town. A line of people waiting for admittance stretched out on the sidewalk behind a yellow nylon rope.

Tulsi gasped. "Look at the line! Maybe we should skip it." Her hand tensed on Lucas's arm. "We'll never get in before closing time."

"Don't worry. My brother-in-law, Sergio, owns the place. The bouncers will let us in immediately." He led her to the front of the line. "Ramon, how's it going tonight?" Lucas shook hands with the four-hundred-pound bruiser of a man standing beside the door at the head of the line. Ramon was also super tall, making Tulsi feel tiny and insignificant as he towered over her five-eight frame.

"Bueno. There's a lot of commotion, and the people keep coming." He looked at Tulsi, still in her bridesmaid attire. "You two go on inside. Enjoy."

The rest of the crowd booed and shouted things in Spanish Tulsi could only guess were insults. Lucas ignored them. They stepped through the deeply carved wooden door into music so loud the bass thudded in her chest, and her heart synced to the beat. Lucas took her hand and tugged her through the thick crowd to the long bar on their right.

"Want something to drink?" he shouted in her ear, motioning like he was drinking from a glass. It was so difficult to hear any conversation that she realized no one was actually talking. Some were standing around cocktail tables and watching the dancers. Most people inside the club were gyrating as if in a frenzy, including those not on the dance floor. They were so thick it was impossible to see who was dancing with whom.

She shook her head, which was good because handling a drink and dancing so wildly would be impossible. "Maybe we should leave?"

His gaze sharpened with concern. "Are you alright? Or is it too crowded or too loud for you?"

"How are we going to dance together in that crowd?" she asked, her gaze straying from his dark eyes to the dancers.

"We'll be fine. But let's wait for this song to end."

He grasped her hand again, and they threaded their way through the throng to the front where the DJ worked. As they got there, the DJ caught sight of them and gestured them over. He grasped Lucas's hand, hugged him close, and slapped his back. Lucas said something in his ear. The DJ nodded heartily and tousled Lucas's thick crown of hair before going back to his equipment. Lucas threaded his fingers through his hair, trying to straighten it. The pounding beat faded in a minute and a lovely slow tune began.

Lucas pulled her close on the dance floor, his hands clasping behind her lower back. Tulsi leaned into him, getting as close as she could, her arms connecting behind his neck. The floor filled around them more than Tulsi thought possible. As the singer crooned in a language she didn't comprehend, she understood by the music that the words were sultry, sexy, and alluring.

The warmth radiating from Lucas set her insides on fire. She wanted this man in her bed. His sexuality and his masculinity were so strong and sure without the usual Latin machismo. She knew he would be a fantastic lover. *And isn't that exactly what I need?*

His hands slipped to her hips, pulling them into his pelvis another inch. The sexy smile on his face let her know he wanted her to feel his erection through the thin fabric of her dress.

Her hands left his neck and cupped his ass. He was too luscious to deny, not that she would consider it. She wasn't sure how long she could wait for this hot man in her bed.

Putting her mouth to his ear, she yelled, "Let's go to my place."

His grin said it all. They weaved their way back outside to the curb and took a cab to Tulsi's condo.

TULSI'S FLAME

In the back of the cab, Lucas pulled her onto his lap. Their lips joined and moved, their tongues seeking and searching. His hand cupped her breast, the thumb pressing into her hardened nipple through the satin fabric. "I can't wait to wrap my lips around it and suckle it."

Tulsi moaned and tried to reach under her bottom to paw at his erection. It wasn't possible, so she squeezed her buttocks together, feeling the stiff rod respond to her movements by twitching up as if seeking a path to the wet font above it. She considered lifting her dress above her waist and sitting on his cock, giving him a wild ride all the way across town. But they were almost there now.

The cab driver must have noted the urgency in his back seat. Tulsi caught the driver's eye in the rearview mirror, though he swiftly looked away. Grinning, he sped down the streets, his eyes flickering to the mirror again and again as if to catch a good show. At two in the morning, with minimal traffic and cooperating traffic lights, it was a quick ride home.

With the cabbie paid, Tulsi took Lucas's hand and led him up to her condo door. She was ready to plunge the key into the lock or break the door down, whichever was faster. The frenzied feeling in her body, accelerated by the club's wild music, had ignited a surging need. She wanted, needed to be fucked, deeply and soundly, as quickly as possible and as many times as Lucas could manage. In her mind, he was in the perfect physical state to keep her coming all night.

The door flew open against their combined weight. Lucas slammed it shut with his open palm and pressed Tulsi against it. His lips devoured hers before sliding down to where his hand held her breast. His teeth teased the hard nipple as his hand cupped her pussy through her gown. Tulsi erupted in an orgasm so strong she saw flickering stars.

Lucas gave a deep chuckle. "That's number one." He peeled off his button-down shirt. "How high can you count?"

"Well over a thousand," she whispered, a smug smile on her face as she turned to let him unzip her dress.

CHAPTER THREE

Blurry-eyed, Tulsi sat up in bed. A rustling noise beside her drew her attention. Lucas was nearly dressed.

"Good morning, beautiful." He leaned over and kissed her. "Sorry, but I've got to run. I'm on duty in half an hour."

"You're going to work in that suit?" He'd put on the same clothes he'd worn at the wedding.

He glanced down at his clothes. "I don't have much choice unless I arrive naked." He winked at her before adding, "I have spare uniforms in my locker at work."

In broad, unfiltered daylight, she averted her eyes and clutched the bed linens to her chest, covering her naked breasts. Heat rose in her cheeks. It didn't matter that they'd had sex most of the night. "What time is it?"

"Six-thirty."

"Yikes!" She jumped out of bed, dragging the sheet with her. "I'm supposed to be at work at seven-thirty."

Lucas met her at the end of the bed. He pulled her into his arms and kissed her so soundly her toes curled into the carpet pile. "Can I have your phone number? I'd like to see you again. Go out on a real date." He pulled out his cell phone and entered her number as she repeated it.

"Give me a call so I have yours," Tulsi said as he started for the door. "Wait! How are you getting there? I thought your vehicle was at the banquet hall."

He turned back. "It is. I texted Dawson. He's coming by to pick me up." He waved and jogged out to the parking lot where Dawson was already waiting.

Despite his asking for her phone number, Tulsi's heart sank. She doubted he'd call. The few guys she had dated never called a second time. Lucas wouldn't either. If her parents didn't want her, why would anyone else?

After her shower, Tulsi pulled on her unisex navy blue scrubs and brushed out her short, glossy, wet hair. Her soft, tawny complexion was even, warm, and so flawless, she never wore more makeup beyond mascara. A quick brush of mascara accentuated her wide-set, large, round, brown eyes. With that done, she grabbed her purse and keys and headed out the door.

She made it to work at the Colby Veterinary Clinic just in time. Not that she needed to be on time to punch a clock. She was a senior staff member even if she'd only been working there less than a week. Still, her appointment book was full and it was the Fourth of July. All hell was bound to happen today.

When she walked to her office, Cortland met her in the hallway.

"Well, cowgirl, how was your evening?" Cortland gave her a saucy look.

"Better than yours from the looks of it." The crumpling of Cortland's face made her immediately regret her retort. It wasn't Cortland's fault Dawson was bailing on her. Bringing up the subject was like rubbing salt into her wounded heart. "I'm sorry. I shouldn't have said that." Tulsi gathered her friend in her arms and held her close. "Maybe he'll come to his senses."

Cortland wiggled out of her grasp. "I doubt it."

Barbra Pari stepped out of her office into the hallway. "Hey ladies, it's the Fourth of July and the phones are already ringing off the hook. Both of you have patients already. Cortland, room one. Tulsi, you're in room four."

Squeezing Cortland's hand, Tulsi said, "I'm serious. He'll come around." The two veterinarians parted in opposite directions.

At lunch time, Tulsi yawned as she walked into her office. Cortland was stretched out on the couch where she had hoped to catch a power nap.

TULSI'S FLAME

"Did you get *any* sleep?" Cortland grinned, obviously fishing for details.

"Not much. I think we stopped after a dozen." Tulsi tried not to smirk, but she couldn't help it. Lucas had been a robust lover. "He must be a firefighter 'cuz he sure knows how to light mine!"

"You hussy!" Cort sprang up and hugged Tulsi tight. "I'm happy for you." She watched as Tulsi pulled off her white lab coat. "It isn't one and done, I hope?"

She shrugged. "He asked for my phone number, and I gave it to him. I also got his. So, perhaps not..." She wiggled her eyebrows suggestively, though she tried not to get her hopes up.

They broke into giggles.

Barbra Pari stopped in at the doorway. "What are you two laughing about?"

Cortland piped up, "Tulsi had a great night. We should be going easy on her today if at all possible."

"Forget about it. We're booked solid, and the appointment phone won't stop ringing." She started out the door before sticking her head back inside the office. "Your next clients are here already, if you want a head start on your afternoon sessions."

The two friends nodded and followed Barbra down the hall to the appointment rooms.

Like passing ships, the two worked, taking their appointments, answering phone calls and questions, and prescribing calming medications for animals frightened by the firecrackers, M80s, and fireworks exploding already.

Andrew's assistant animal control officer, Gordon, called asking for help as the sun went down and all hell broke loose with pyrotechnics. Cortland went to the shelter to care for the animals as they came in, leaving Gordon free to follow up on runaways and missing dogs. Tulsi stayed at the clinic in case emergencies arrived.

During Cortland's absence, Tulsi had to field all calls and see any patients brought into the clinic. Everyone wanted either Cortland or Hannah instead of her. She was the new vet, unknown to them. Explaining that Hannah was on her honeymoon, and Cortland was out assisting the Colby Animal Control mollified some, but others abruptly decided to forgo coming to the clinic.

One client in particular was rather rude. An older man, Mr. Becket, brought in his anxious chicken. The neighborhood kids had chased the poor creature, throwing firecrackers at it. When Tulsi entered the room, the man went tense.

"I asked for Dr. Woodbridge," he grunted, his hen clutched tightly in his arms. Sensing his alarm, the animal started clucking wildly, trying to escape its owner's hold.

Tulsi stayed back, unsure what to do. "I'm sorry, but she's on her honeymoon right now, and Dr. Stewart is out on a call. I'm the only veterinarian here at the moment."

"We'll wait for Dr. Stewart, thanks." He sat down in the appointment room chair. The hen got a wing free and started flapping it, trying to flee.

"Is your hen hurt?" Tulsi decided to ease into the examination, thinking he might relent.

Reluctantly, the man replied, "She's upset, is all."

"Do you have any beer at home?" She leaned against the door, her arms crossed over her chest.

"Yup, I was drinking one when the ruckus started." Mr. Becket looked at her funny. "Are you allowed to drink on the job?"

Tulsi bit back the retort she wanted to give. Instead, she said, "I suggest you bring your hen home, pour a shot glass of beer, and let her drink it. It'll soothe her ruffled feathers and calm her down. Just make sure it's not too much, otherwise, you'll have a drunk chicken on your hands."

The man's face flushed red. "I will not give Marietta beer. She's a good hen and I don't want to kill her."

"Mr. Becket, I would never suggest anything that might harm your hen. I promise. It's an old farmers' tip."

"From where? India? I'm not stupid, and I don't like your suggestion. I'll bring my girl out for a long ride. Maybe that will calm her down." The man scowled at Tulsi before stomping out of the exam room.

Tulsi understood Mr. Becket's response, although she didn't like it. They were familiar with the vet staff, and she was new. She'd barely been there a week before Hannah's wedding. Not nearly enough time to prove her abilities. Still, the lack of trust irked her and fed into her insecurities. Especially with species she hadn't worked with in years.

It was well past midnight when the two veterinarians got together back at the clinic.

"You look beat," Cortland said to Tulsi as she entered the front door. "Why not try to take a nap in your office?"

"I tried. Several times." Tulsi knew she looked like crap. She felt like it, too. Her eyes were red and puffy, and her energy level had slumped lower and lower as the night went on. Barbra had grinders delivered from Roberto's, along with sodas and a tray of cookies to keep the entire staff functioning. The food and caffeinated drinks helped Tulsi regain her energy for short sprints of time. She should have remembered all the work likely coming today and gotten more sleep last night. Shaking her head, she decided her night with Lucas was worth it.

The two friends worked together the entire weekend, catching naps here and there. At one point, Barbra blocked out an hour in the appointment books for each to sleep.

About noon time on the sixth of July, Cortland and Tulsi got a text message from Hannah. She and Andrew were on their way back to Colby. Tulsi replied, telling her to take the night off but to be prepared for chaos in the morning. While the major fireworks explosions had subsided, firecrackers and bottle rockets in backyards were still spooking pets.

Tulsi hugged Cortland. "You're looking pretty sad, what's going on?"

Cortland rolled her eyes. "I went searching for Dawson. He and his fire crew were handling a brush fire at the high school soccer field. He drove past your car, but I'm not sure he recognized me."

Tulsi hugged her tighter. "Aww, I'm sorry. I know this has been tough on you, seeing him after your breakup and all. But I have faith everything will work out for both of you. Give karma some time to figure it out."

"Karma," Cortland huffed. "Well, I leave on the first flight out tomorrow. If she's going to intercede, I hope she works quickly." She sank down on Tulsi's office couch. "I saw Lucas too. Driving the truck."

Tulsi's face brightened. "How'd he look?"

"Handsome and a little tired. I bet the fire department has been going all weekend, too."

Tulsi's chest warmed with the mention of him. "He is exceedingly handsome. You should see him without clothes on." She shook her wrist to indicate he was too hot to handle. The thought of their night together made something in her lower belly all warm and mushy.

"Oh my, what are you going to do?"

She shrugged. "Not sure. But if I do anything, I'll wait until after tomorrow. We both need to catch up on some sleep before our next encounter." *Assuming he called her at all.*

CHAPTER FOUR

Captain Dawson Michaels approached Lucas as he sat at Station Two's kitchen table. From the dark circles around his eyes, Lucas could tell he was just as tired as he was, maybe more so. This holiday weekend had been brutal on the fire department. Every station had been called out on what felt like hundreds of brush fire calls. "Why so glum?" Dawson asked as he sat down across the table from Lucas.

"I'm trying to figure something out." He looked at his friend and boss. "Should I or shouldn't I bother to apply for the lieutenant's position when Korth vacates it?"

Dawson rubbed his chin. "Why wouldn't you?"

"I've only been in the department two years and I don't have as much experience as some of the other guys who also could apply." Lucas drummed his fingers on the tabletop.

Dawson sat back in his chair. "You've all been through the same educational and practical training sessions. But you know what?"

Lucas's eyes latched on to the captain's face. "What's that?"

"You have more going for you than most. You've lived in this town for what, twenty years? You know it...every street and every business. Most of the others came from outside town, some from other states."

"That can't mean anything to the selection committee."

"Don't underestimate anything. Plus, you have one other thing going for you that the other candidates, except Dixon, have. You are a minority."

Lucas shook his head. "I don't want to play that card. If I'm going for the job, it has to be based on my experience, education, and, most of all, merit."

Dawson leaned forward, putting his arms on the table. "I don't think your DEIA card will get you the job. However, it might tip the scale if you're tied with someone else for the position." He wagged his index finger at Lucas. "I think you will make it based on knowledge and experience alone. But you can't win the promotion if you don't try."

Lucas's throat went dry. "So you think I should go for it?"

"Absolutely. Take the written test. I think you'll ace it, along with the physical agility test. Let it come down to an experience game. You might not win this time, but the test results hold for a year." Dawson's name was being called from somewhere in the apparatus room. He stood to leave. "Don't forget, my captain's position will become vacant when I leave. Any current lieutenant will be able to apply for that promotion. And *that* will give you a second chance at a promotion."

"Huh, I hadn't considered that." Lucas nodded, a burst of confidence erupting in his chest. "I guess I will apply. What do I have to lose?"

"Nothing at all," Dawson said before disappearing beyond the apparatus bay door.

CHAPTER FIVE

Days passed and still Lucas didn't call. It was just as well because Tulsi and Hannah were so busy taking care of residual appointments from the holiday weekend that she hadn't had time to think about him. Well, not much anyway. She was eating her lunch in her office between appointments on Tuesday when her phone rang. Seeing his name pop up on the phone screen had her squealing with delight.

"Hi," he said. "Remember me?"

Tulsi couldn't help but smile. "Yeah. Thanks for calling."

"I figured it was a good sign when you answered since you'd already know exactly who it was calling. How have you been?"

"To. The. Wall. The phone calls and the patients haven't stopped coming. I'm so glad Hannah is back, though it's too bad Cortland returned to Alaska. I was hoping the three of us could spend more time together before we split up again." She paused a second to think of something else to say. "How did the holiday go for you?"

"I managed to do my own shift and a couple of extras. There were a lot of brush fires throughout town, thanks to a week without rain before all the fireworks."

"Ugh, don't I know it. The clinic phone was ringing off the hook, and people were begging us to give them something to calm their critters. The hard part was that I've been out of the loop with treating domesticated mammals, so I had to constantly check with Cortland about dosages."

"I don't understand. Aren't you a full vet?" Lucas asked softly.

"Yes, I'm a fully trained veterinarian, but I spent the last two years exclusively treating reptiles and other exotics. It was my specialty in vet school. My former employer wouldn't let me do anything else." It didn't escape her notice that choosing to work with exotic species, combined with her features, made people think she was exotic too.

"Reptiles? Snakes?" Lucas's voice held incredulity. "Do they have ears? Can they hear?"

"Snakes and turtles don't have ears, so they can't hear. They feel low-frequency vibrations, which most fireworks don't make. Nearly all reptiles have some hearing, but like snakes, they rely more on vibrations."

"Huh," Lucas said. "That's amazing. What made you choose that specialty?"

"My baby brother had all kinds of reptiles during our childhood. They were the only pets we were allowed to have: caged and silent."

"I grew up with dogs and cats and a few guinea pigs. Well, not including my four siblings."

The number took Tulsi's breath away. "Five total? It was only my little brother and myself. I can't imagine five." She sat back in her desk chair and fiddled with her half-eaten sandwich. Her lunch break was nearly up but she didn't want to end her conversation with Lucas.

Lucas laughed. "It was a mad house. Total chaos. And no privacy whatsoever. It didn't help that the house is a small Cape with only three bedrooms, one for my parents, one for the boys and one for the girls."

"How many of each?"

"Three boys, including me, and two girls. I remember my mother's parents, trying to help my mother care for us. They only ate native Puerto Rican foods, and every Puerto Rican cultural holiday was celebrated in the traditional manner. All us kids are bilingual because they only spoke Caribbean Spanish. Both our parents speak a mix of English and Spanish at home. With the rapid fire of our speech, it can be hard to decipher at times." He shrugged. "How about your family?"

"My parents adopted me when I was three years old. They were having fertility issues. But as often happens, my mother got pregnant with my brother, Thomas, a year after they adopted me. It's been the four of us ever since." Tulsi didn't usually tell people her story. For some inexplicable reason, she needed to tell Lucas.

"Wow. I can't imagine. Do you know anything about your biological parents?" He quickly added, "If you don't mind my asking."

"Nothing, really. I have my adoption papers. They list my birthday and the name of woman who surrendered me to the orphanage. That's all I have."

"Have you ever tried to locate your birth parents?"

He couldn't see her shaking her head vehemently. "No. I wasn't wanted. Why would I want to give them the chance to reject me a second time?" Her words came out a little more irritated than she wanted. "If they want to find me, they can."

"Oh." Lucas went silent.

"Anywho, I have my adoptive parents and Thomas. That's plenty enough for me."

A soft knock on her door, before it creaked open. Barbra Pari must have seen she was on the phone because she tapped her wrist to indicate the time. Tulsi nodded silently, and Barbra disappeared behind the closing door. "Hey, I'm sorry to break off our chat, but I have a client waiting."

The silence on the line returned until Lucas stuttered, "I—I actually called to ask you out on Saturday night. Dinner?"

Tulsi's insides warmed. "I'd like that. Tell me where and when."

"Mind if I pick you up at seven?"

"That sounds great."

The remaining week slowed, intentionally, Tulsi thought, because she was so looking forward to seeing Lucas again. She didn't have any idea where they were going. Her text message requesting more information had gone unanswered. She didn't think much of it because she knew there was a big fire in the south end of town. The entire Colby Fire Department and four neighboring towns had been fighting it for three days. She worried that Lucas wouldn't be able to break away for their date.

Right on time, he knocked on her door. When she opened it, he stood there in figure-fitting jeans and a navy, short-sleeved polo-style shirt. "Wow, you look magnificent," he said.

The sight of his bare, muscular arms made her heart skip a beat. Tulsi could feel the blush rising up her face, setting fire to the tips of her ears. "It's only jeans and a casual shirt," she said, glancing down at her clothes. "I didn't know what to wear."

"Red is definitely your color, and I like how the jeans cling to your legs. They're pretty gorgeous, you know." Lucas stepped over the threshold.

Unable to think of anything to say, she settled for, "Thanks."

"Sorry I didn't reply to your text messages. That furniture warehouse fire was a monster. It was all hands on deck for the last three days."

She motioned him inside. "I can't even imagine. I remember what happened to Dawson."

Cortland had told her about Dawson's injury and how he sustained it. A captain in the Colby Fire Department, he'd been trapped by falling debris inside a burning building. Luckily, he had been rescued just as his air pack ran out. He was still limping from a broken ankle. A departmental investigation revealed that Lieutenant David Korth had failed to refill the air pack tanks. The department was going through the process of firing the lieutenant for the negligence that nearly caused a firefighter's death.

Remembering the incident made Tulsi's knees rubbery. It wasn't lost on her that Lucas could have experienced the same fate that day and could do so at any call he went out on. It chilled her. "Do you get frightened at those kinds of calls?"

"Fire like that is unpredictable and scary. Firefighters have to focus on doing their job. Fear causes paralysis, which can get a firefighter killed." Lucas walked purposely over to the hallway. He stretched up and pushed the smoke detector's test button on the ceiling. Nothing happened. "I was afraid of that." He shoved his hand in his pants pocket, pulled out a nine-volt battery, and proceeded to install it in the detector.

Tulsi joined him in the hallway and watched as he swapped the batteries. "You didn't have to do that."

"I most certainly did. They don't work with dead batteries." He walked back to stand beside her. "This complex is a disaster waiting to happen. If there's ever a fire, it will go up faster than dried pinecones."

Tulsi couldn't believe her ears. She'd taken over Cortland's lease and hadn't lived there very long. "Really? How can you tell?"

Lucas pulled her over to the window to look out at the building across the parking lot. "See the roofline? It's all one piece. That means there's no firebreaks. It's also likely one big open space in the attic area."

"Firebreaks? What are those?"

Lucas leaned against the window frame. "It's usually a masonry structure between building segments. Its purpose is to stop a fire from spreading from one section of the building to another. Stop the fire from extending. The buildings in this complex pre-date building codes that require firebreaks, so there aren't any." He looked her squarely in the eyes. "If there's ever a fire anywhere in this complex, get the hell out of your building quickly."

"I'd lose everything?" Tulsi couldn't believe the buildings were such a fire hazard.

"Probably." He took her hand and said, "So get out quickly and get your neighbors out, too."

"My neighbors don't like me."

His face took on a surprised look. "Why not?"

It was a tough subject. Should she come right out and accuse them of being racist? Tulsi shrugged. "If I had to guess, it's my skin color." Uncomfortable with the tangent the conversation had taken, she glanced at the wall clock. "What time is our reservation?"

Lucas checked his watch. "In fifteen minutes. Let's go."

CHAPTER SIX

Tulsi liked Pascoe's restaurant immediately. For one, it wasn't Roberto's, where she and Hannah usually ended up when they went out for dinner. She liked Italian food as much as every other American, but sometimes the service was less than attentive, and the food offerings never changed.

Pascoe's was set in a colonial house built in the 1720s. The brass and crystal fixtures and polished oak woodwork in the bar area gleamed under the dimly lit wrought iron chandelier. Old pictures and antiques were displayed as historical evidence of the three hundred-plus years the structure had stood. Its menu of award-winning New England fare could be ordered in the quieter side rooms or in the more relaxed bar area. At one end of the bar section, a fireplace blazed with a real wood fire, giving the entire large room an intimate ambiance and a subtle smoky aroma.

After ordering their meals and drinks, Lucas asked, "I know you mentioned your family before, but you didn't say where you grew up."

"I was born in New Jersey. The Anthonys adopted me. I grew up in their Chilton, New Jersey home. It was your usual small town. Lots of gossip and nosey neighbors. Everybody knew everybody else. Some people like that sort of fish-bowl environment." She took a sip of her pinot grigio. "Personally, I couldn't wait to get the heck out of there."

"Why's that?"

The familiar lump formed in her throat. She sipped at her drink, trying to ease the pain before continuing. "The town had no more than four hundred residents. I was the only non-white person in that small town. I stuck out like a knife in someone's back."

"Yikes, that's pretty bad. Were you teased or bullied because of your skin color?"

"Oh yeah. Some of it was very subtle. Those microaggressions were so subtle you might not catch it when it happened. Other times, it was blatant." She returned his hard gaze. Seeing his slowly nodding head, she added, "You know what I mean." It wasn't a question. Anyone who was remotely different, especially in skin tone, was automatically considered an outsider, regardless of their birthplace.

Lucas nodded. "Absolutely. We used to live in a small town in Florida. Terrible place to be non-white. People never let you forget you don't look like them. And because of that, you don't deserve a good life."

"Exactly." She swirled her wine glass, watching the wine's legs dribble down the inside of the crystal goblet. "When it was time to go to college, I beat it the heck out of there to Rutgers University. Being in such a diverse student body and faculty was amazing."

Talking about Rutgers made Tulsi's heart lighten. It had been one of the most profound experiences in her young life. Being accepted as American by most students despite her external appearance. Being free to be who she was, without question, had allowed her to consider a happy future. That was why she loved being there so much, and it nearly broke her to leave after graduation. "From there, I went on to vet school at Cornell University. That's where I met Hannah and Cortland."

Their food arrived, and they continued talking during their meal.

Lucas stared at her a few moments as if he was thinking hard.

She stopped chewing and swallowed so she could talk. "What's on your mind?"

His head cocked, he said, "So you're adopted."

It wasn't a question. Just a statement repeating the fact she'd let slide. "I was, but I'd rather not discuss it now." At the look of horror in his eyes she quickly added, "It's not an awful subject. Please don't feel bad for asking. I don't want to discuss it tonight. That's all."

His eyes held hers. "I understand. Another time." He pushed a few remaining French fries around his plate before asking, "What made you choose to specialize in reptiles?"

"I don't really know. I guess I always felt bad for them. Most people don't like reptiles or amphibians. To me, they're fascinating. Snakes, turtles, frogs, iguana, geckos. You name it. They're all so different. And usually misunderstood and improperly treated by their owners. One client didn't realize her son's bearded dragon needed UV-D light. It nearly died. I try hard to teach owners how to care for their special pets so everyone can stay safe and healthy."

"That's admirable. And yet, you don't have any pets."

"No. Pets take time and attention, especially reptiles and exotics. More than most people realize. Until I'm settled, I'll stay pet-less. When my life is in order, I'll adopt either an emerald tree skink or a gecko." She shrugged while staring at him. "What you told me about the condo building has me a little un-nerved. I'm not sure I want to worry about leaving a pet there." Talking about the possibility made her insides quiver, and not in a good way. She took a sip of wine and changed the subject. "What about you? Any pets?"

"Gosh, no. The house is still full of chaos. My younger brother and I are the only ones still at home. My older brother and my sisters are all married, most of them with kids already."

Tulsi blinked rapidly. "You still live at home?"

His pained expression said it all. "Yeah. Considering my work schedule, it hasn't made sense yet to move out. I'm saving most of my paycheck for a house. One of these days, I'll buy one."

Tulsi set down her fork, her mind reeling. Then she remembered where he worked. "Ah, you're on that weird firefighter schedule. What is it…twenty-four hours on, then forty-eight off? Right?"

"Exactly. It would be hard to have a pet if I couldn't be home for twenty-four hours." He shrugged one shoulder. "Plus, there's mandatory overtime and extra shifts. Not to mention the major fires where everyone is called in until its under control. Some take days, like that furniture store warehouse earlier this week."

"So what will you do? Get a roommate or ask your brother to join you?"

"God, no, not Marco. I probably wouldn't mind a roommate." He gave her a funny grin. A grin, Tulsi decided, that could mean anything from, "hey, you want to be my roomie" to "God, help me find the right roommate."

The waitress arrived with the check. Tulsi reached for it, but Lucas was faster. He pulled out his wallet.

"Let's split it," Tulsi suggested.

"Nonsense," Lucas said, handing the waitress his credit card. "I asked you out to dinner, remember?"

"Yes, but it's 2024. We *can* split the check."

The waitress returned his credit card and receipt.

"Not tonight," Lucas said and looked up at her expectantly. "Ready?"

They walked out of the restaurant hand in hand, stopping at the passenger door of his bright red pickup. It gleamed under the parking lot lights.

"Nice truck, by the way."

He patted the vehicle fondly. "I keep this baby cleaner than the trucks at work. And that's saying something because we wash *them* every day."

She instantly compared it to her father's pickup. He'd never cleaned it, inside or out. Certainly not by himself. He'd always paid the detail shop across town to do the dirty work. Tulsi liked that Lucas took care of the things he loved. "You're welcome to do mine any time." She chuckled. "I don't think it's washed more than once a year."

Lucas slapped his palm over his heart and stumbled back a step dramatically. "Sweetie, show your car some love. That's atrocious."

"I know, I know. I never think about it, except when I bring it in for an oil change with a free car wash." She leaned back against the door and looked up.

Lucas leaned back beside her. "What are you looking at?"

"It's such a nice clear night for stargazing." She pointed. "That star there, the one with the red color. I think that's Gamma Draconis."

"Huh," Lucas said. "You could tell me it's a black hole, and I'd never know the difference. Would you like to go somewhere we can see better? Someplace without the lights?"

Goose-pimples rose on her arms as a warmth swept through her middle. His interest in pleasing her was so unlike her few previous dating experiences. "Sure."

Lucas opened the door for her and helped her in. When she placed her hand in his, he didn't let it go. "I—I want you to know I'm not expecting to..." His voice trailed away. "You know..."

Tulsi laughed. "So it was that bad?"

He shook his head vehemently. "No, no, not at all. It was great. I don't consider it a foregone conclusion every time we have a date." He scuffed his shoe against the asphalt. "I fully intend to leave you at your condo and go home tonight."

"Well, so you think." She gave him a stern look. "Maybe *I* have my own plans."

His eyes sparkled, and a small upturn at the corners of his mouth spread warmth through her core. He shut her door and hopped into the driver's seat.

They drove in silence to the outskirts of town where the high school was located. Behind the school were the soccer and baseball fields as well as the track. A faint odor of smoke hung in the air. The soccer fields were dark with soot, the remains of the grass fire over the Fourth of July weekend.

Tulsi slipped her hand in his as they walked silently to the middle of the field. The moon, only a thin crescent tonight, wasn't throwing off enough light to interfere. "Outside of Ithaca, we could always see a million stars and the Milky Way on clear nights."

"I've never looked at the skies much. It is beautiful." Lucas stared at her. "And you're beautiful." The squeeze of her hand let him know she heard him, though it was several minutes before she looked at him.

"Thank you. I find you very attractive, Lucas." Her voice came out low and husky, like the first words out of one's mouth on first awakening.

They gazed into each other's eyes. He could feel the pull of her. He knew what was coming. Her head tipping up ever so slightly gave him permission. And he didn't disappoint her.

His lips brushed against hers, feeling the softness, their plumpness as he supported her head in his cupped hand. He reached around her waist with his free arm, pulling her flush to his body.

When her lips parted and her tongue darted out against his lips, he groaned and deepened their kiss. They went at it hot and heavy until Tulsi broke it off.

"You are a great kisser," she whispered.

"Thanks, so are you."

They leaned forward until their foreheads met. A lock of her hair brushed against his cheek. Its silkiness made him remember running his fingers through it and then down the soft skin of her neck. Lucas closed his eyes, relishing the light floral scent of her hair…sweet, spicy, and fragrant. He inhaled and opened his eyes to find her own staring at him. "Your dark eyes. They're so expressive."

She pressed against him. "What are they saying?"

He chuckled softly. "They're begging me for more kisses?"

She sighed and lifted her forehead from his. With regret in her voice, she said, "They are, but I have to work the early shift tomorrow. Would you mind if we ended our evening?"

He'd been close to ignoring his plan. Her request made sense for both of them. He shook his head. "No, not at all. I could use a good night's sleep after this last week. I have to work tomorrow, too." He gave her a devilish grin. "You'll have to owe me a rain check."

Her eyes widened as she sputtered. "Rain check? What for?"

"You said you were going to seduce *me* tonight." His eyes twinkled in the limited moon light.

"Any other time," she said as Lucas slipped his arm around her waist, and they headed back to his truck.

Lucas drove her home the long way, taking roads running along the outskirts of town. Their hands tightly clasped between them, they rode in silence. He didn't want their evening to end so soon.

"Thanks for a great night. I like getting to know you," Lucas told her as they stood outside her condo door.

A hoarse cough brought their attention to a middle-aged woman approaching up the sidewalk.

"Good evening, Mrs. Rasper," Tulsi said brightly, a sweet smile on her face.

The woman answered with a scowl as she passed them, unlocked her door, and disappeared inside.

Her smile fading, Tulsi asked, "See what I mean?"

"Ignore her. She's of no consequence."

Tulsi seemed anxious all of a sudden. She wrung her hands together as if not knowing what to do. Lucas tried to change the subject. "Oh, I can't believe I didn't tell you the best news. That lieutenant's position opened up. I've taken the exam and passed."

Tulsi's face brightened. "That's great! So you got the job?"

He shrugged. "Not quite yet. There's two other applicants. We have to go through an interview. The committee will decide."

Holding up her hand, she crossed her fingers. "I hope you get it." Her eyes roamed his face as if waiting for him to say something else. "Well, I should get inside. Have a good shift tomorrow."

"Thank you. You too." He rocked on his heels before adding, "Would you like to go out again sometime?"

The way Tulsi's grin exploded wide across her face made him think she was hoping he'd say that. "I'd love to."

Lucas's insides got bubbly and warm again. "I'll give you a call tomorrow to see what we can work out."

Tulsi nodded.

He leaned into give her a peck on the cheek, not trusting himself to leave if he tasted her lips again.

When he backed away, their eyes held. She whispered, "Be safe."

"Always."

CHAPTER SEVEN

The back door of his parents' house banged open as Lucas hustled out the door the next morning. *What the heck am I making for meals today?* He tossed his overnight bag in his fire engine red pickup truck. It was nearly six-thirty a.m., and he had to stop at the grocery store to get the ingredients for today's breakfast, lunch, and dinner. It irked him he hadn't given it any thought before now. But he couldn't have after that kiss last night. His mind, his senses, and the ache in his chest were all centered on Tulsi.

Shifting his thoughts to his kitchen duty, the vision of her, her hair's floral smell, her soft lips lulled him back into last night's date. That kiss, God help him, her lips, her mouth, he wanted to kiss her into infinity. The thought made his knees feel squishy, like he was walking on a smoldering wood floor ready to give way beneath his feet.

"Shoot." He steered his focus back to food again. Breakfast. "I think it'll be hash, eggs, toast, and a fruit salad." Saying the words out loud made it easier to concentrate on the task at hand, which was planning the damn firehouse menu. Something that should have been decided long before now. "Lunch—"

"Lucas!"

He looked up to see the petite figure of his mother in her hot pink fuzzy bathrobe at the back door. She stepped out on the stoop, her hands waving him to come back. Gray strands in her otherwise dark brown hair glinted in the early morning light. He rolled down the window. "I don't have time, Mama. I have to get to work. I'm going to be late."

"Lucas Campbell-Lopez, you come back here. You didn't come home after the wedding , and you've been gone all week." Her eyes narrowed. "Where were you?"

He got out of his truck and stood on the edge of the driveway. "Mama, I'm a grown man. Do I need to tell you everything?" He rolled his eyes to heaven. Really, talking to his mother about his night with Tulsi was not on his playlist.

"Yes. I brought you into this world, and you live under my roof. You owe me an explanation. It's been a week since that wedding. Have you been avoiding me?"

He lied, "I was too drunk to drive, so I stayed at the firehouse. It was close to the wedding venue. And we've had extra shifts to cover over the holiday weekend. And then there was the warehouse fire—"

His mother held up her palm. "Enough." She crossed her arms over her chest. Pouting, she glared at him but remained silent as if she were assessing his answer. He could tell she didn't entirely believe his alibi. But unless she had some kind of proof, she wasn't going to harp on the subject.

"I have something important to tell you." Her heavy Puerto Rican accent trilled across the driveway. "Come here."

Heat rose in his chest. He knew if he didn't return immediately, she would argue with him loud enough for the entire neighborhood of McMansions to hear. They were already a spectacle for the neighbors. The last time they argued out in the yard, the police had been called by the lady next door.

He knew his mother wouldn't stop until he returned to her. It saved precious time and effort to just obey. Growling softly, he went over to the concrete steps. White paint was peeling off the door frame, adding to his elevating blood pressure. Juan was supposed to paint the trim on the house this summer, yet he'd made no plans or at least hadn't shared any. Lucas tamped down the anger rising in his gut. "What?"

She pointed her finger at him. "Don't you forget, tomorrow you are expected here for dinner. Don't you be making any other plans." She shook her index finger at him sternly. "No overtime."

Lucas closed his eyes. "You know I can't turn down extra shifts. We're short-staffed." He glared at her. She knew he was low on the grunt list. And she knew he wanted to replace former Lt. David Korth.

Turning down any extra shifts would not look good during his upcoming interview.

"I don't care. I arranged for Melena Gomez and her parents to come for dinner. You will not disappoint me."

He scrubbed his hand through his hair. "Mama, I am not interested in your matchmaking. I will find my own bride when it's time to marry."

She planted her fists on her extra wide hips. "You will be there tomorrow, or, God help me," she crossed herself swiftly before uttering, "you can move out."

Whoa. She'd never threatened him like that before. He'd been evading her matchmaking since moving back home over two years ago. She was turning up the heat on him when he was trying to focus on the lieutenant's position. "I will do my best, Mama." He headed back to his truck.

His younger brother came racing out the back door, dodging his mother. "Wait up! Can I borrow your truck?"

His mother added to the chaos, yelling from the house, "Get Marco a job at the firehouse."

Lucas ignored her demand and focused on Marco. "What do you need it for?" Marcos never asked to borrow his truck. He knew Lucas would want a detailed report on why and where he was going with it. Unless needed for picking up or delivering large things, Lucas made it clear the answer would be negative. This instance had to be for something special. Still, the quivering in his gut suggested he should say no. He'd worked long and hard to afford the vehicle and didn't trust anyone—family or otherwise—to drive it.

"I need to pick up something at Willard's Hardware. It's too big for Mama's car."

Lucas paused, assessing the request. "You'll have to drop me off at work and pick me up in the morning." Sternly, he added, "And don't you dare scratch that truck, not even the bed."

Marcos veered around him and got in on the passenger side. "I'll take care of your baby."

"You better," Lucas growled as he backed out of the tiny driveway, the needed grocery store trip forgotten.

He fumed over his mother's demands during the entire ride to work. The idea of getting married, or even engaged now, made the acid in his empty stomach churn. He wasn't ready to settle down. Moreover, he wanted to pick his own cariñito. A flash of Tulsi's smiling face, the sultry "come here" look she had given him the night of Hannah and Andrew's wedding, erupted in his brain. She was divine. He had wanted to take her out for another date tomorrow night. A choice would need to be made.

Was his mother's threat sincere? Or was it a bluff? If need be, he would move out. The downside would be not being able to save as much money for a house of his own.

If he didn't work overtime, he would have to make an appearance at his mother's dinner. Like all the other arranged dinners, he'd smile and be pleasant but distant. Melena Gomez was a nice girl. She'd been raised with the same strict upbringing as his sisters. Puerto Rican women were expected to be docile, meant for marriage and children, while men were powerful, aggressive, and heads of the household. At seventeen, Melena was a little too young for his twenty-nine years, as far as he was concerned. Last time he saw her at a church event, she'd had an outbreak of pimples.

He pulled into the firehouse parking lot, praying he'd have a mandatory extra twenty-four hour shift tomorrow morning.

Grabbing his overnight bag, he tossed Marco the truck keys. "I've been having a little trouble with the electrical system. If the power windows go up and down on their own, turn off the engine. It should be fine when you restart it."

Marco gave him a salute. "Aye, aye, Captain." Seconds after Lucas shut the truck door, Marco revved the engine and peeled out of the firehouse parking lot. The bad feeling in his belly made Lucas instantly regret agreeing to the truck loan.

CHAPTER EIGHT

"You're exceptionally quiet today," Bob told Lucas, breaking the silence between them at the firehouse's kitchen table. "Did you not pass the written and agility tests for Korth's position?"

"Oh, I did. I'm waiting on the interview with the selection committee. It's later this afternoon." Thinking about it, Lucas's jaw tightened. He'd done well on both tests, while all but three had washed out of the application. The competition was fierce. Any one of them might win the coveted position.

It had been a trying morning. Lucas had arrived at the firehouse without the groceries he was supposed to pick up on the way. Not that he'd figured out the rest of the menu yet. Last he remembered, he was thinking about lunch when his mother cross-examined him about the night he didn't come home. The sensational night he'd spent with Tulsi.

He and Bob had darted off in the rescue truck to pick up meal supplies at the supermarket down the street. Once there, Lucas decided on a corned beef theme. Reuben sandwiches for lunch, and corned beef with the fixins in the crockpot for dinner. The only downside was the sauerkraut. It would stink up the kitchen as it simmered. By tonight, the upstairs bunk room would reek with the sharp-smelling fumes.

This morning's conversation with his mother echoed in his head. She was hell-bent on finding him a wife. Over the last two years, she'd paraded over a dozen young ladies before him, hoping he'd find one interesting. It never worked. They all seemed like insipid, giggling nitwits. How could he even consider spending the rest of his life with someone like that?

On the few occasions he did consider marriage, Lucas wanted one like his parents. They had married for love. Actually, they were crazy for each other. They still got along well, like a united force of nature that poked and prodded their children toward success. Maybe it was because his father traveled extensively for work as an airplane maintenance inspector. How could they fight when he was never home half the time?

"I've a lot on my mind." Lucas picked up his coffee mug to take a sip. A dribble slid out onto his work shirt as he tipped his cup. Grabbing his napkin, he tried brushing it off. It sank into the sturdy denim fabric, leaving a stain. He flung down his napkin, shaking his head. Today was not going well. He refocused his thoughts on their conversation. "You're married. What's it like?"

Laughter erupted from Bob, his shoulders shaking, a hand over his mouth as he guffawed. "You thinking about marriage?"

Lucas shook his head. "My mother's been after me for years to find a girl and settle down. I don't think I'm ready for that. She keeps pestering me, playing matchmaker to get me married." He knew in his heart that his mama wanted him settled with her definition of a *nice* girl. Nice meant a Puerto Rican girl. After what happened with his last girlfriend, he understood her motive. That didn't mean he liked it.

Truthfully, from the example his parents presented, marriage looked good. They each brought their own strengths and weaknesses to the union. It was clear to him, as it was to the rest of his family, immediate and otherwise, that Graham Campbell and Carmen Lopez not only loved each other, they were best friends. He wanted that kind of relationship someday. A strong bond of friendship before the vows. Having been raised Catholic, it went without saying that divorce was not an acceptable option. Even if the church allowed annulments, a fracture like that in the family would not be taken favorably. His mother would never forgive him.

Bob crossed his arms and leaned forward, resting his forearms on the tabletop. "My wife and I get along okay."

"But are you friends?" Lucas emphasized his words by tapping his index finger on the wood surface.

"We've been together for ten years, eight of them married, so I'd say we were friends. Not close, mind you. But we had a mutual attraction.

Our backgrounds mirrored each other." He sat back in his chair. "Don't get me wrong. We argue often. I'm home more now that our shift schedule changed. She expects me to help with the kids and chores. I don't always do things the way she wants, which leads to heated discussions. But overall, while I'm not sure I'd do it again, it's not bad."

Lucas considered marriage to be a trial by fire. Fire, he understood. Women, not so much, despite having two sisters. "Hmm. No glowing review there." Lucas leaned forward and whispered, "I'm not sure it's for me."

The look of shock on Bob's face made Lucas backpedal. "It sounds hard."

"It is. There's a lot of back and forth, disagreement and compromise. You know what they say about marriage?"

Lucas's eyes opened a little wider, and he leaned closer. "No, what?"

"You'll know when you're ready."

Bob's anticlimactic words only brought more confusion to his state of mind. "Great," he deadpanned.

With his bad luck with relationships, would he ever be ready?

Lucas thought of Tulsi. It was too soon to tell if she was the one. Regardless, he wanted to take her someplace special. Not a movie or dancing again. Not yet anyway. What was there to do in Connecticut in the middle of July?

Trip to Watch Hill or Block Island? A whale watch? That might be interesting, but he didn't know if Tulsi got seasick or not. SailFest in New London? It was this coming weekend. He had to figure something out and run it by her since she might be on call.

The sounding alarm disrupted his thoughts. The PA system blurted out the specifics. Car fire in the parking lot of the lumberyard, about eight blocks away.

He and Bob jumped out of their chairs as the bells continued chiming. It was time to roll.

Lucas put his gear on and jumped into the side compartment. The Pierce fire engine jolted forward as Jennifer, one of two female firefighters, drove it out onto the street. Usually, Lucas or Bob drove the rig, but as a new recruit, she was still in the driver training phase. Today, he and Bob were working as deckies, handling the hose lines and the attack.

The engine bumped along the city street, cars pulling over to let them pass. The truck came to a screeching air-brake halt in the Ace Hardware parking lot, where a vehicle was fully engulfed. Black-brown acrid smoke roiled from the pickup truck, engulfing the vehicle in ten-foot-high flames.

Lucas jumped down and pulled the redline, a one-inch diameter red hose, toward the vehicle. It was hard to discern what make of truck it was. Minutes ticked by as sixty gallons per minute of a foam and water mixture soaked around and under the charring vehicle until the flames relinquished their hold. The blackened pickup dripped water and foam into a large puddle.

With the fire out, the small crowd gathered to watch the excitement thinned. Lucas and Bob began re-packing the hose in the fire truck to return to the station. Bob fed the wet hose up to Lucas in the bed on the top of the apparatus. They needed to bring it back to the station and hang it in the hose tower to dry. Dry hose would be stacked in the empty hose bed, ready for the next call.

"Come on guys, we haven't got all day," Jennifer said, leaning against the side of the rig watching them, her arms folded over her chest.

"Jen, you could help," Bob replied, motioning to Lucas up in the hose bed. "You'd fit up there better than either of us."

She stood to her full six-two height. "Not my assignment today."

"Lucas," a weak voice called from below him.

TULSI'S FLAME

He turned and looked down. It was Marco, standing beside the engine. Lucas climbed down off the engine. "Hey, I thought you were going to Willard's?"

Marco's face was pale. "They didn't have what I needed, so I had to come here." He glanced at the smoldering hulk of a truck. "I'm sorry. When I parked, the windows started going up and down like you mentioned. I shut the engine off like you suggested, and when I started it again...I don't know what happened."

His rapid-fire Spanish mixed with emotion was hard to understand, even for Lucas. He followed Marco's gaze to the burned vehicle. His breath caught, his heartbeat racing as he blinked rapidly. He glared at his brother, who wouldn't meet his eyes. "Are you saying—?"

Marco shrugged, his palms up in bewilderment. "I don't know...it was weird. I smelled this funny acrid odor, and in the next second, smoke was pouring out from under the dashboard."

The bottom of Lucas's stomach fell as he approached the hunk of carbon. Walking to the back of the vehicle, he stared at the license plate. With his glove, he rubbed soot off the metal plate.

His heart stopped. It was his truck.

CHAPTER NINE

Hannah stepped out of examination room three, shutting the door behind her. She leaned against the wall and closed her eyes. Her hand fanned her scrub shirt as if she needed to cool herself down.

"You okay?" Tulsi whispered, placing her hand on her friend's shoulder. It was Sunday afternoon, and they both were busy with so-called emergency cases that could have waited until normal appointment hours.

Hannah's eyes flashed open wide, her hand rising to cover her heart. "God, you scared me."

"Sorry. I didn't mean to startle you like that. I saw you standing there in silent repose, looking, well, frankly...miserable."

Hannah turned and leaned her right shoulder onto the wall. She waved her hand to bat away the sentiment. "Sometimes I wish I only had to deal with the clients' pets and not the clients." She sighed heavily. "Just another owner who can't stop feeding her dog into obesity, heart disease, and an early death."

"I know. I see it all the time, too. And then we get blamed for her dog's early demise." Tulsi rubbed Hannah's forearm. "Maybe we could focus on that issue in our next clinic newsletter?"

"Good idea, I'll ask Barbra to write it up." Hannah pressed her lips together and nodded. "Summertime is a good time to remind owners their dogs and cats shouldn't be eating picnic or barbecue foods."

"A reminder during the Thanksgiving, Hanukkah, and Christmas holidays might help, too."

Flashing her index finger at Tulsi, Hannah said, "I'm glad we're discussing the newsletter. I need you to write a short article for the next edition."

"What topic?"

TULSI'S FLAME

"You need to introduce yourself and promote your special skills as a reptile, amphibian, and exotics veterinarian." Hannah ticked each subject off on her fingers.

"Could I add basic care for reptiles? It's a universal problem, especially with new owners." She paused before adding, "Back in Louisiana, I wanted to start an exotic pet support group. Of course, they said no. Perhaps I could start one here once we're fully staffed."

"I think there's a bunch of owners out there who would value your help with that, but let's hold off on the support group idea for now. Do include that information in your newsletter write-up."

Tulsi's enthusiasm dampened, but at least Hannah hadn't said no to the group idea. Getting word out about caring for reptiles and exotics had always been her dream. She definitely saw a need, no matter where she worked. "How long should my introduction be?"

Hannah brightened. "The part about you can be one to one and a half pages long. The reptile tips, no more than a page to start. You can always reserve space for another go at it."

"Can I view previous copies to get an idea of the format?"

Hannah slung her arm around Tulsi's shoulders. "Of course. The latest edition is on the website. Barbra has previous editions if you want a broader perspective. Which reminds me to ask Barbra to leave space in another newsletter to introduce Frances. Once she gets here."

"Frances." Tulsi rolled her eyes. "Good idea."

Hannah stood up straight and lowered her voice. "Do you have a few minutes? There's something I'd like to discuss with you." At Tulsi's nod, they retreated to Hannah's office. She flopped down in her rocking chair and gestured for Tulsi to sit on the couch.

Hannah's rocking was swift and furious as her white-knuckled hands clenched the arms of the chair. "I ...oh hell, I don't know how to tell you this." Hannah jumped out of the chair as if launched and started pacing the small office.

"Just spit it out." Thoughts of what Hannah might say spun through her mind like a Ferris wheel revolving at full speed. Maybe it had something to do with Frances Mueller. Did their former classmate decide not to come work with them? "Is this about Frances?"

Hannah's nose wrinkled. "No. Well...sorta, but not really." Her pacing picked up speed. "I didn't say anything earlier, before the wedding. I thought my period was late because of all the nuptial stress and being worried about Cortland."

Tulsi's hand covered her mouth, a deer in the headlights look on her face. "Are you pregnant?"

The frightened look on Hannah's face said it all. "I thought...we thought Andrew was sterile. He told me he was. We used condoms while dating. But we kinda got out of the habit when we were living together." She scrubbed her face with her palms and slumped into the rocking chair again. "Anyway, I took a pregnancy test on our brief honeymoon."

"Oh my God. I can't believe it." Tulsi knew Hannah wasn't interested in having children. Her friend had often told her she didn't want to bring a child into the world and fail to give it a good life. "Does Andrew know? He—" The desperate look on Hannah's face shocked her even more. Cautiously, she asked, "It is Andrew's, isn't it?"

"I can't believe you asked me that question!" She jumped up again and started pacing. "It can only be Andrew's baby. I didn't tell him. I don't know how to tell him."

Tulsi watched as Hannah went to the window and gazed into the back parking lot. "Do you have any idea how far along you are?" she asked gently.

Still looking out the window, Hannah shook her head slowly. "No. Maybe a couple of months, no more."

"Have you had any morning sickness or other signs?"

Again, Hannah shook her head. "I've been tired. Wicked tired. That's nothing new since I bought this clinic, though. But otherwise, nothing."

"Hmm, it could have been from all the drama with Cortland and Dawson and the wedding planning on top of all that."

"Yeah. I keep hoping it's a false alarm. But I don't believe it is. That positive line on the test stick was pretty dark."

Tulsi's voice lowered to a whisper. "If it's true, are you going to keep it?"

Hannah's face crumpled in misery. "I couldn't have an abortion. You know that's not how I am. It wouldn't be fair to Andrew. He needs to know if I am pregnant."

Slapping her knees, Tulsi rose from the couch. "I think he'd be thrilled to the moon and back. Especially after thinking all this time he was infertile. He's so great with his nephew, Daniel, and his niece, Erica. He'll be a wonderful father."

A smile slowly crept onto Hannah's face. "He *will* be over the moon." It quickly faded. "I'm not sure I can do it."

"What? Be pregnant?" Tulsi stood beside her best friend.

"No—yes." She groaned. "I'm not sure I can go through childbirth. It's going to hurt big time."

"Yeah. I've heard it's no picnic. But hey, look at all the women who have babies. They're okay with it afterward. Most have more than one. It can't be too bad." She put her arm around Hannah's shoulder. "You and I have watched animals in labor, we've done cesareans on them. We know how it works and what to expect."

"That's not going to make it any easier. If anything, I'm more scared to death about it."

Tulsi squeezed her shoulders. "I understand. I would be, too." She paused. "I'd say the next step is to be sure. Can you get in to see your gynecologist?"

She shrugged. "I don't have one. I wonder if Cortland's dad knows anyone good here in Colby." Cortland's father was a doctor in the West Point area of New York, about three hours away. Cort's mother was a gynecologist, but she was the last person Hannah would ever contact.

Hoping to soothe her mind, Tulsi pulled Hannah into her arms, hugging her fiercely. "I'll do some asking. See where other women are going. Who they might recommend."

"Not here." Hannah's eyes widened. "Don't ask the staff. They're too astute. They'll immediately think it's me."

"They might think it's me." Tulsi chuckled, flicking her eyebrows up and down.

Hannah erupted in giggles. "True. I heard you and that firefighter were pretty tight on the dance floor at the reception."

Just the mention of Lucas made Tulsi's insides warm and gooey. "True. He's one hot firefighter."

"You two hook up?" Hannah's tone was cautious. "I'd hate to see you go through what Cortland's going through right now."

"I know. After we left the reception, we went to a dance club."

"And—?" Hannah looked better now that she had changed the subject. A pink hue had returned to her cheeks, and her eyes sparkled. Or was that because of the salacious discussion?

Tulsi's ear-to-ear grin said it all. "We did." Hannah's gossipy enthusiasm made her giggle. "We've had another date since then, though Lucas behaved like a total gentleman. On purpose."

"Ha! I'm glad for you. Enjoy yourself, but don't get hurt like Cortland." Hannah looked at her watch. "My next client should be here any minute." She turned to check her image in the mirror on the back of her office door. "I know I don't have to ask, but I'm still going to. Please don't say anything to anyone until I'm sure."

"You got it. In the meantime, I'll gather some names and check all the credentials online. I should have a list of names in a few days. How's that for a plan?"

A knock on the door interrupted Hannah's reply. The door cracked open an inch. It was Valerie, the lead vet tech. "Both of you have clients waiting. Hannah, room two, Tulsi, room four."

"Coming," Hannah said. When the door was closed again, she turned to Tulsi and said, "Good plan. Let me know."

On the way home later that evening, Tulsi contemplated Hannah's predicament. If she was pregnant and decided to go through with the pregnancy, Tulsi would be holding down the clinic during her maternity leave. With Frances Mueller as her only help. God only knew if Frances would be of any help, considering how she'd acted at Cornell.

Frances was due to start in two weeks. Tulsi was not looking forward to working with her. Yet, she would give the woman the benefit of the doubt. Perhaps during the two years they had been out of vet school, Frances had worked someplace that straightened out her attitude.

Tulsi's cell phone rang as she pulled into her parking spot at the condo. "Hello?"

"Tulsi. It's Lucas. How was your day?"

Warmth started building in her lady parts. "Not too bad. Lots of clients and their owners. How was your day?"

"Well, um, not good. Not good at all." His heavy sigh followed his words. "Long story short, my truck caught on fire. It was totaled."

Her breath caught in her throat. "Oh, Lucas! Were you hurt? What caused it?"

"No, I'm not hurt. I lent it to my brother, Marco. He was with the truck when it burst into flames. I was on the responding fire engine."

"Oh my God, you must have been frantic!"

"Actually, I didn't recognize my own truck underneath all that flame and charred metal. After the fire was out, I saw Marco at the scene, and he broke the news to me." He was quiet for a few seconds before adding, "It most likely started in the electrical system."

"I'm so sorry. Is there anything I can do?" She felt awful for him. Not only losing his beloved truck but also being the one to put the fire out and discovering it in that manner.

"Nah, I called the insurance company. They're giving me a free loaner. A Honda Fit."

He didn't sound pleased about it. She decided to focus on a positive note. "It's great you have a loaner. Even if it is something less than optimal for your masculine lifestyle." She quickly added, "I heard those are one of the best small cars."

"I heard they don't make them anymore." His flat tone made it clear he wouldn't be interested in buying one even if the model was still available. "Hey, I was wondering if you wanted to go to dinner tomorrow night? You'll have to drive."

She glanced at her watch. "Not a problem. Should I pick you up?"

"Would you mind terribly?"

She shook her head even though he couldn't see it. "No, of course not. Text me your address."

CHAPTER TEN

The address Lucas texted to Tulsi surprised her. Sparrow Street was in a posh housing development on the far side of town. It was incongruous with his description of living in a small Cape overcrowded with siblings. Did he falsify his description, or was his family's home at the edge of the McMansion development?

She pulled up outside the Dutch blue-painted Cape. The only description she could think of was well-worn. The clapboards needed a paint job, as did the white trim. The front lawn appeared well cared for, lush and dark green, if maybe a tad long. Perhaps the mower was due any day now. She steered her SUV into the driveway, parking behind the older model Escort and alongside the newer-looking Chevy. There wasn't a Honda anywhere in sight. *Is he home?*

Should she go to the door or wait for him in her vehicle? The unease in her gut had her staying put for a few minutes. *Looks like I'm going to have to suck it up and go to the door.* She paused a little longer and changed her mind. Snatching up her phone, she texted: 'I'm in your driveway. Where are you?'

After hitting send, she waited with her eyes glued to the screen.

She jumped in her seat when someone knocked on her car window. There was no way this wasn't his mother. The same brown hair, but hers streaked with gray strands, her oval-shaped face was lightly wrinkled, and her eyes were the darkest brown, almost black. Her chin was cleft, and her head peeped over the window edging. Tulsi rolled down the window. "Hello."

"Are you waiting for someone?" The woman crossed her arms over her ample chest. Her khaki cotton shorts were as baggy as her tunic top.

Tulsi nodded. "Lucas. I'm here to pick him up."

The woman gave her a dubious look. "He's not home."

"I sent him a text message. Let me see if he responded." Smiling faintly, she picked up her cell phone. There was a reply from Lucas.

Tulsi decided it was best to read it aloud. "He says, 'Stay where you are. ETA less than five minutes.'"

Mrs. Campbell's nostrils flared. "Let me see that." The woman held out her hand.

Tulsi didn't want to give it to her. Lucas had also written something personal. Something she didn't feel comfortable sharing. Certainly not with his mother. She whipped her head around, hoping Lucas would be driving down the street. While she was distracted, Lucas's mother snatched the phone out of her hand and stepped away from the SUV.

"Oh, please. Give that to me." Tulsi bolted out of the vehicle and followed the woman, her hand held out, begging for it.

Mrs. Campbell glared at the screen, her eyebrows pinched and her lips pressed together. "'Can't wait to get you naked in my arms again.'" She glared at Tulsi. "Huh," was all she said.

Just then a car horn honked. It was Lucas in his loaner vehicle.

Both women watched as he sped down the street. He slammed on the brakes, his tires screeching as the car abruptly halted in the driveway. Lucas jumped out. "What's going on?" He glanced from one to the other with a hard look blazing in his eyes.

• • • •

His mother planted her hands on her hips and advanced on Lucas. "This perra says she's here to pick you up."

"She has my phone," Tulsi interjected.

"Mama." He held out his hand, and his mother slapped the phone into his palm. Lucas handed it back to Tulsi, whispering, "Can you wait in your car while I straighten this out?"

As Tulsi turned toward her SUV, Mrs. Campbell stepped toward her. "No, no. Introduce the puta." His mother crossed her arms over her chest defiantly. "She must be the one you stayed with after the wedding." Giving him a satisfied smirk, she added, "I wasn't born yesterday, Lucas."

"Mama, enough."

"Lucas—" She gave him a death stare, her tone brooking no disobedience.

He rolled his eyes. "Mama, this is Tulsi. Tulsi, this is my mother."

The two women glared at each other.

Lucas's blood pressure spiked again. "Okay, enough." He grasped Tulsi's hand and led her back to her car. Raking his hand through his hair, he said, "Get in the car. I'll be right back."

Tulsi gave his mother a backward glance before she did as asked.

Relieved that at least Tulsi was willing to de-escalate the situation, Lucas returned to his mother. "Must you be so unpleasant?"

She shrugged. "I didn't know this person sitting in my driveway. With all the trouble we've been having with the neighbors, I needed to see who it was. Besides, Melena and her parents are coming for dinner in an hour. You can't leave, not with her." His mother gestured toward Tulsi.

He put his arm around his mother's shoulder and walked her to the back door of the house. "You asked Melena and her parents to dinner. I didn't."

"Lucas. Campbell. Lopez. Don't be a cabron. You are not going to stand up Melena."

He opened the door, letting his mother walk through. "No, I'm not. Because I didn't ask her to dinner. I have other plans tonight." He pushed the door shut and turned to walk away. The click of the door latch alerted him his mother had opened it again. He turned back and stared hard at her. "Deja de hacer un escándalo. The neighbors are watching."

She glanced up and looked at the houses across the street. The three houses on the other side had their front doors open, their occupants watching them. Seeing he was right, she reached to close the door. "We will discuss this later. Don't think otherwise."

Lucas breathed a huge sigh of relief as he retrieved a small shopping bag from the rental car. Running late, he feared something like this would happen. He got into Tulsi's SUV and slammed the door shut. When Tulsi jumped, he was immediately sorry and squeezed her hand. "I'm sorry I was late and sorry my mother gave you so much trouble. Let's get out of here."

"She didn't like me." Tulsi's eyes looked watery.

"Don't cry." Lucas squeezed her hand again. "Trust me, she doesn't like any woman that isn't Puerto Rican."

Tulsi closed her eyes and exhaled hard, her shoulders slumping further. "Great. Not only do people not like me because I'm not white, now more don't like me because I'm not Puerto Rican."

"Forget about it. Let's have a good evening together from this moment on."

Tulsi stared at him as if he'd slapped her. "Easy for you to say. You weren't called a puta." Her face flushed red as her shoulders stiffened. "I know what that means. All my life I've been treated like an outsider. Unwanted from birth all the way to today."

He took her face in his hands and gently wiped away her tears. "I want you. My mother and the rest of my family are going to love you once they get to know you."

"Sure." Tulsi's eyes rolled as she shook her head.

He kissed her cheek. "Let's go. Head toward Mystic. I'm taking you to the aquarium and then to dinner."

"It's open late?" She backed out of the driveway.

"Tonight, the jellyfish exhibition opens under black lights so we can see all the different colors they fluoresce." Lucas leaned over and kissed her cheek again. "You're going to love what I have planned."

Her jaw dropped, and her eyes widened in surprise. "Oh my God, Lucas. That sounds amazing. Thank you!" She leaned over and kissed his cheek.

Lucas chuckled. "Let's go, or we're going to be late."

CHAPTER ELEVEN

The aquarium overflowed with people. Between the children who raced through the crowd and the strollers, Tulsi was having difficulty controlling her temper. All it would take was one adolescent to knock over an elderly person and disaster would ensue. Either a laceration, bruise, or possibly a broken arm or hip.

In the fading light of the July evening, they wandered the outside exhibits, hand in hand. The seals, walrus, and beluga whales fascinated Tulsi. Watching the animals took her mind off the scene at the Campbell house. It was her and Lucas. Just the way she liked him.

"Have you ever worked with aquatic animals?" Lucas asked as they paused longer than normal at the Steller sea lion enclosure.

She shook her head. "Not mammals. Turtles and frogs, yes. We didn't have the opportunity at vet school. There were a couple of aquarium post-doc programs, but I had already decided on reptiles, amphibians, and such. This makes me wish I had applied to a few of those programs anyway."

They continued walking, heading for the African penguin pavilion. Because of the crowds of children, they didn't linger.

"I understand they have some reptiles and amphibians too. In the main gallery." He took her hand.

Tulsi's heart raced, sending a stream of warmth through her body. It was so thoughtful of Lucas to take her somewhere he knew she would enjoy.

They toured the main gallery building, seeing all the exhibits, including the jellyfish. The brightly colored jellyfish fascinated the attendees as thoroughly as the penguins and sea otters had.

Tulsi noticed Lucas kept looking at his watch. "Do we have a reservation time?"

"Yes, but not the one you think. If you've seen everything here you want to see, I have another surprise for you."

They walked back to the admissions area, where Lucas made contact at the special events window. The woman nodded as Lucas grasped Tulsi's hand again. "We follow the tour guide."

"Where are we going?" Tulsi asked, trying to figure out what kind of reservation Lucas had made.

"We're going on a behind-the-scenes tour. I told them you're a veterinarian in nearby Colby, and they managed to find someone on their vet team to show us around."

They spent the next hour visiting the on-site veterinary hospital and the off-exhibit animal enclosure. The rehabilitation area for stranded and sick animals as well as rescued sea turtles fascinated them. Tulsi's heart thudded with excitement as she toured the site, asking all manner of questions, especially about the hospital and sea turtles. The veterinarian who took them around was animated with her, and while Lucas didn't understand some of what he was hearing or seeing, he seemed to enjoy that Tulsi was in her element and thrilled.

In a blink, the tour was over. Before they parted, the tour guide, Dr. Eckart, made arrangements for Tulsi to return at her leisure during normal hours to speak with the reptile veterinary staff.

She turned to Lucas and hugged him tightly. "That was amazing," she gushed. "Thank you so much. I can't believe they want me to come back and talk with them about their reptiles. What an incredible opportunity to collaborate!"

• • • •

Her exuberance stirred up a warmth in his chest for having given her an experience she had enjoyed immensely.

"That's all I have up my sleeve for tonight," Lucas said as they exited the aquarium. "Except dinner, of course." He was pleased with himself for thinking of the aquarium and eating in downtown Mystic. It was a beautiful, calm night, and not too hot since the sun was setting.

They drove into downtown Mystic, arriving in time for their late dinner reservation.

The hostess led them to the patio, now lit with strands of fairy lights. Their table overlooked the Mystic River with a great view of the drawbridge connecting the Groton side of the town with the Stonington side.

The food and drinks were delicious. Lucas noted Tulsi acted less animated than previously. A full belly and two beers? Or was it too much excitement for her in one day? "Are you tired out?"

Tulsi shook her head. "Yes, and no. The aquarium was outstanding. I can't thank you enough for bringing me." She glanced away, turned back to him, and looked as though she were going to say something, but took a sip of her beer instead.

Lucas's nerves remained on edge. She obviously had something on her mind and he had a hunch what it was. He leaned over the table and whispered, "What's on your mind?"

She looked at him, her fingers fiddling with the formerly ice-frosted glass now dripping rivulets of cold water. Picking up her napkin, she wiped her hands. "I have two questions, but I'm not sure if I'm overstepping."

He waved his hand as if pulling her forward. "Go for it. What are they?" He crossed his forearms and rested them on the table.

"This is about your parents' house. It's out of sorts with all the other houses on Sparrow Street."

He sighed. "Yeah. Back when my parents bought the house, it was surrounded by beautiful forests and farmland. When the farmer died, his next of kin sold the land to a developer who promptly gentrified the area, building all those oversized houses. It became a posh neighborhood surrounding my parents' house. The developer tried to buy them out, but my parents refused to sell." He crossed his arms over his chest. "The neighbors don't want us there. They covet and re-imagine this neighborhood as exclusively their own. Puerto Ricans are not desirable neighbors, according to them. Our tiny, well-worn Cape is so out of place now, it hurts their property values."

"But you were there first!" Tulsi sputtered.

"They easily forget that and the fact it was there when they were picking out their lots and signing mortgages." He leaned back in his chair. "What's question number two?"

"You and your mother had some words...in Spanish. She looked angry."

His gut hunch was right. "My mother invited some friends over for dinner, hoping to fix me up with their daughter. I was ordered to be there. Frankly, I forgot after the disaster with my truck." He picked up her hand and caressed it. "I didn't want anything to do with that matchmaking. I only want to spend time with you." He squeezed her hand.

She was silent a few moments, her smile tentative at first but disappearing. "I didn't make such a good impression with her."

"My mother is very protective of me." He decided to be honest with her. "Of all my siblings, I'm the only one who is interested in someone who isn't Puerto Rican, and my mother can't stand it."

• • • •

Tulsi's breath evaporated. Once again, she was being singled out or, in this case, left out and rejected for her ancestry. She couldn't believe, in this twenty-first century, she would have to continue to deal with the issue over and over and over again.

Lucas caressed the palm of her hand. "I'm sorry I was so blatantly honest. Are you okay?"

She nodded, blinking rapidly to stem the tears stinging her eyes. "Yeah, I'm okay. I should be pleased you're interested in me, but if it fractures your relationship with your family, are you sure you won't regret it?"

"Of course not. My mother is frantic to have me married off. She's been putting together these matchmaking dinners for more than two years, hoping to spark a romance. I avoid them as often as I can."

"But your heritage, your culture..." Tulsi started, her brow furrowed and her eyes darting wildly.

"But then I met you." He kissed the back of her hand, sending shivers up her arm and into her chest. "I'm perfectly happy to spend time with you. I wish we could be together more but I'm being on my best behavior at work."

She raised an eyebrow. "Why is that? The job opening?"

"Yeah, for the lieutenant's position vacated when David Korth was fired. I passed the written and agility tests. I had my interview yesterday afternoon after we got back from my truck fire. I'm waiting to hear from the selection committee."

Leaning forward, Tulsi placed her hand on his. "Did the interview go well?"

Lucas blushed. "Well enough. I was hoping they'd cut me some slack. Instead, they had a great time ribbing me about putting out my own truck fire." He scratched the back of his head. "Still, it seemed to go okay."

"Do you think you're going to get it?" Tulsi asked.

"They were pleased I know the town so well. I've been living here for years, so I'm familiar with the streets and the different businesses in town. Even though I've been in the department for only two years, all my training has been exemplary. I'm not sure if I got the promotion, but they seemed to have a positive attitude about my application."

Tulsi knew Dawson Michaels was captain on the same shift Lucas was on. "Is Dawson on the committee? Can he put in a good word for you?"

"He's not. He won't be around much longer, so he was not appointed to the committee. He did give me a great reference."

"Not going to be around?"

"Didn't Cortland tell you? Dawson is leaving for a new job in Ohio."

Her eyes popped wide. "Ohio? Not Alaska?" Everything came together in her mind. Cortland was seriously bent out of shape about something after the wedding. She returned to Alaska as soon as Hannah was back from her honeymoon.

"Wow! That explains Cortland's rapid exit out of Colby." Tulsi couldn't believe Cortland hadn't said anything. Her heart must have been broken if Dawson chose Ohio over being with her. "When does he leave?"

"There's less than a week left to his notice. His going away party is at the Irish Harp on Friday night."

Tulsi made a mental note to contact Cortland as soon as she was free. Steering her thoughts back to Lucas, she asked, "You expect to hear soon?"

"Yes. They've had three applicants. I haven't been in the department for as long as one of them, but I'm hoping." He held up his hands, all his fingers crossed. "I aced the written test. There's several minorities in the department, including a few Puerto Ricans, but we're mainly all truckies, or deckies. No Puerto Rican has ever held an officer's position at Colby Fire Department."

She nodded. "You're going to break that streak. You deserve to get whatever it is you want."

"Speaking of wanting... what do you say we go back to your place?"

A wide grin erupted on her face. "I thought you'd never ask!"

Back at her condo, Lucas tuned the radio to a Latin music station. While Tulsi got them drinks, he gyrated about the living room. When she tried to pass him a beer bottle, he swept her into his arms and danced her around the room. "We should go over to El Fuego again some night. Next weekend is a Bomba festival."

TULSI'S FLAME

"I don't know how to dance in that way." Tulsi broke free of Lucas's embrace and set their beers down on the side table. "You should teach me something, but not tonight."

Lucas tuned the music to a classical instrumental station. "Right, I just want to chill with you in my arms." He dropped to the floor and gestured for Tulsi to join him.

They made out on the carpet before the flickering gas fireplace, shedding items of clothing one piece at a time. It was slow and sensual this time rather than wild and urgent.

She let her fingers brush along the contours of his arms, feeling the smooth, taut muscles of his pectorals and down to his eight-pack abs. "You must work out pretty hard," she whispered, reveling in his gasps, sighs, and low moans as her groin ached for him.

"You like what you see and feel?" Lucas whispered in reply, his voice raspy with desire.

"Yes, it turns me on."

He started to get up, but her hand on his chest stopped him. "Not yet. I have more to explore." His grin widened as he lay back.

Tulsi explored his body with her tongue, finding spots that made him groan or sigh with pleasure, which gave her a throbbing sense of control and satisfaction. "Roll onto your stomach," she said. Lucas complied, giving her more to explore. She found he liked having her tongue flick at the base of his spine, right where the cleft of his buttocks started. The end of his cock, visible between his legs, lengthened and jerked with pleasure and anticipation.

"Your turn," Lucas announced, sitting up. He removed her lacy bra and panties then guided her onto her stomach. As she had done, so did he. His tongue teased and licked her back from the nape of her neck to the start of her cleft. The entire time, her moans and sighs of pleasure seemed to spur him to continue.

The teasing awakened every nerve in her, igniting flames over her body. She could feel her arousal. Her pubic area felt swollen, hot, and wet, ready for him to take her to the next level. He dallied before spreading her thighs and crawling between her legs. The press of his cock between her buttocks jolted her. "Not that," she called out, rising in a push-up.

Realizing what she meant, he replied, "I had no intention. Relax and enjoy the sensations." He rocked forward and back, sliding his cock, slick with her juices, over the crack of her ass.

Her heart galloped as she lifted her behind with each thrust over the surface of her buttocks. "Lucas!" She groaned, wanting him to take her, fill her, and give her sweet release.

He stopped and sat back on his knees. "One more side." He reached for the foil packet, quickly donning the condom.

She swiftly turned over, hoping to accelerate to the good part. The parting of her swollen pussy folds and the stretching, the filling of her vagina. Her channel was hot and aching, waiting for his cock to bring her over the edge.

Instead, he started kissing her face, her eyes, her nose, her jaw, before leaving a trail of kisses and nibbles down her neck. His tongue played with her erect nipples, flicking and sucking. Her moaning was continuous as each touch of his tongue sent shivers throughout her body. Her fingers entwined in his thick hair, nudging him lower.

At last, he complied. His tongue flicked across her clit. It was like throwing lighter fluid on a roaring fire. She dug her fingers into his hair and exploded in a powerful orgasm.

• • • •

Lucas stroked himself, aching to enter the tightness, the heat of her wet chamber. When Tulsi roused from her climax, he stroked his cock between her folds, listening to her exultations, feeling the incredible pleasure with an anticipation only she had ever brought out in him. When his balls ached, he couldn't wait any more. He entered her to the hilt, then stayed still. He felt the velvety walls of her pussy quivering against his engorged cock.

She thrust her hips up, sinking him deeper. The thrust shattered his patience. He pounded into her, hearing her scream with pleasure as her vagina tightened, clenching hard around his cock in orgasm. He let loose, shooting a stream into the condom sheath.

As their breathing and pleasure settled, Lucas looked at her in amazement. This woman, so docile dealing with an adversary but so aggressive with sex. If her fire in bed could only be harnessed to stand up for herself when needed most, she would be invincible. Lucas wanted to make it his mission to help her.

CHAPTER TWELVE

The next morning, Lucas offered to make breakfast sandwiches with egg, sliced deli ham, mustard, cheddar cheese, and wedges of fresh tomato, and she accepted enthusiastically. After a night of great sex and the deep sleep, her body and brain felt fluid, unable to focus.

Tulsi took a bite, closed her eyes as the flavors hit her tongue, and slowed her chewing to savor every bite. "Lucas, you're a genius. I didn't think I had anything for breakfast other than cold cereal or a hardboiled egg."

"For nearly eight years, I worked as a short order cook when I got out of high school in Sergio's first business, The Colby Diner." He grinned. "It didn't survive, but that's where Sergio and my sister, Arely, first met." He took a bite of his sandwich before adding, "I think the only reason the fire department hired me in the first place was to be the station cook. 'Rattlin' the pans' is what the firefighter brotherhood calls it."

"You cook at the firehouse?" She had never thought about it. "Doesn't everyone bring their own meals?"

He chewed rapidly and swallowed hard after taking a bite of his sandwich. "Some stations or shifts do that. My shift, we usually develop a menu, and pitch in for food costs."

"Sounds like a lot of extra work."

"Ah, but that's the gist of it. I don't have station chores because I do all the cooking. I don't have to do the dishes either." He flashed her a smug smile.

"Lucky you. I have to bring lunch every day or order delivery to the clinic. I'm told the pizza joint down the street sometimes surprises us with pies. The owner is a client." She popped the last bite in her mouth and glanced at the clock. "I have to get going. I want to get to work early to check on a surgery patient."

He brushed his hands free of crumbs. "Got it. Overstayed my welcome." He feigned a sad pout and rubbed his eyes with his fists like a child.

"Nonsense. You are always welcome here." She wrapped her arms around him, turning his frown into a warm smile that sent ripples of pleasure through her. "Give me a kiss and hug, and I'll see you whenever."

Lucas did as he was bid, hugged her tightly, and gave her a lingering kiss. "I'm on duty tomorrow. I'll call if I get a chance. Scratch that...when I get a chance." He opened the door, pantomimed tipping a hat, and disappeared.

Her cell phone rang moments later. Tulsi grimaced when she glanced at the caller ID.

"Tulsi, you haven't called in weeks! Is everything okay? Are you all right?" Her mother's voice blared over the speakerphone.

"Hey, Mom, I'm fine. How are you?" Tulsi sat at the kitchen table and sipped her cold coffee.

"We haven't heard from you. Your father and I are fine. What's happening with you?"

She piled the breakfast plates and utensils and deposited them in the sink. "I've been busy at work. In fact, I'm heading over there now to check on a patient."

"Are you driving? Tulsi, you know better than to talk and drive." Her admonishing tone set Tulsi's teeth to grinding.

"No, but I'm heading for the door. Everything is fine. I've been busy working."

"Have you met anyone?"

She knew what that meant. Her mother had her old-fashioned way of thinking that a woman could have a career, but her main purpose in life was to marry and raise a family. Her father wanted her to keep to the American norm. College and work were fine for his girl, but marriage and kids were the ultimate goal. "Mom. Please leave my non-existent love life out of it."

Her mother tsked. "I want you to be happy, dearling. Your father and I are happily married and we only wish the same for you."

Tulsi scowled at her mother's words. She knew the truth, and what her mother was not saying. More than once, her mother had told her to "marry a nice white boy." The unspoken addendum was "No one else would do for our daughter."

More than once, she'd asked her parents why she should marry a white man. Her mother had said they were trying to watch out for her interests. They didn't want her to struggle with her identity all her life. Tulsi pointed out she was struggling anyway, and she always would struggle against bias and racism. Marrying a white man would not change the color of her skin and the negativity other people hold when seeing her.

Despite their feelings on the subject, Tulsi wanted to keep her options wide open. She saw herself as an American first, a veterinarian second, and somewhere, far down the line, as someone of Indian ancestry.

She remembered her mother and father's looks when her junior high prom date arrived to pick her up. They were appalled to meet her date, a boy of Indian ancestry. The next day, they lectured her on how she deserved a full-blooded, white American boy of Anglo-Saxon heritage. It didn't matter that Zak was born in the United States and fully Americanized, just like her. While they denied her accusation, she knew that as a girl of Indian ancestry, they saw her as a lesser person than a full-blooded white American-born child. Unlike her younger brother, Thomas. Their only biological child.

"If you're being defensive, it must mean you have." Her mother's voice went stern. "Please tell me he's white."

Tulsi hated the fact her parents were both psychologists. Every phrase she had uttered throughout her life was filtered through their psychology-laden brains, searching for a hidden meaning. They were always telling her it didn't matter if she was adopted; they loved her regardless, which had the opposite effect on Tulsi. Nearly every day, she heard that message, which made her feel less and less accepted each time. And now this. She refused to answer her mother.

She heard her mother cup her hand over the receiver and call for her husband in a muffled voice. "Tulsi's dating someone." Her regular strength voice came back on the phone as she asked breathlessly, "Tell us all about him. You're on speaker so your father can hear the news."

Her father's cheerful voice called out, "I'm here, my curry girl. Who did you meet?"

She hadn't been called by that nickname in so long, the abruptness nearly brought her to her knees. As a young child, she found it funny. That was before she realized what "curry" meant. Why couldn't they see she identified as a American woman, not as the South Asian Indian that her skin, hair, and eye color externally identified her as.

"Dad, don't call me that. Please," she groaned. Since recognizing their racism, she had tried to dissuade her father from calling her that. Despite a PhD in Psychiatry, he didn't understand that it was like picking a scab off a wound to rub salt in it.

In all her experience, she knew denying the relationship would not deter her parents. They were able to sniff out the truth despite her protestations. "I met him at Hannah and Andrew's wedding. He was a groomsman. He's nice. A firefighter here in town."

"Oh, a big and brawny type. He sounds wonderful!" The glee in her mother's voice was unmistakable.

Lucas was not what her adoptive parents would like to see their daughter dating. Rather than try to correct her mother's faulty image of Lucas, she said, "Hey, I've got to go to the clinic. I'll call you later tonight. Okay?"

"Sure, dearling. We'll wait to hear all about your firefighter boyfriend."

Tulsi hung up the phone, not waiting for the usual goodbyes, love-yous, and talk-to-you-laters that always dragged out the ending of a phone call with them.

Stunned by the turn of the phone conversation, she remembered her Asian American fifth-grade teacher. The woman had been a proponent for women, enticing all her students, both male *and* female, to seize every opportunity to build a life for themselves. That teacher's words resonated with Tulsi. They allowed her to not just dream, but to dream big. She knew she probably wouldn't be where she was today without that advice.

She showered quickly, got dressed in her scrubs, and hurried out the condo door. Her mind tried to focus on her waiting in-house patient but it kept falling back to her evening and night with Lucas. The memories warmed her to her toes. With fluttering in her stomach, she couldn't wait to hear from him again.

Tulsi was on a mission when got into the clinic that morning. "Here," she said, dropping a piece of paper on Hannah's desk.

Hannah picked it up. Staring at it, she asked, "What's this?"

"The names I promised to get for you. I put them in order, best to last."

Hannah lowered her voice to a whisper. "OB doctors?"

Tulsi nodded as she turned to leave. "Yup. Good luck. Let me know." she said as she strode out Hannah's office door.

"Thank you!" she heard Hannah yelling as she shut the door behind her.

CHAPTER THIRTEEN

Tuesday morning was more hectic than usual with the early arrival of Frances Mueller. While she wasn't officially working yet, she stopped in to fill out the last of her employment paperwork.

Tulsi walked out of the examination room after looking at a bearded dragon. The initial reason given was ADR, short for "ain't doing right." This was its first vet visit, so the reptile was not cooperative. It took one look at Tulsi and started bobbing its head, bearding, and hissing. At one point in the exam, it tried to bite her. Fortunately, Tulsi had a lot of experience with the species, so she acted before suffering a painful bite from its sharp teeth. The newer owner had a lot of questions about some of the antics he had observed. Tulsi was able to calm the owner's fears, explaining the position was called pancaking. A bearded dragon gets as flat and large as possible to help regulate its body temperature since it is cold-blooded.

Hannah approached as Tulsi leaned against the wall, trying to write her notes about the dragon. Someone was walking two steps behind her. "Dr. Anthony, you remember Dr. Mueller from Cornell?"

Frances stuck out her hand, and the two former classmates shook. "It's great to see you again, Tulsi. I'm looking forward to working with you and Hannah."

Tulsi looked her up and down. Frances was wearing overly fashionable, expensive clothes: a leather miniskirt, fishnet stockings, three-inch heels, and a see-through white blouse with a plunging neckline that revealed a lacy, black bra. Topping it off, her face was heavily made up with rouge, fake eyelashes, and black eyeliner that reminded Tulsi of a Goth look. She gave Frances a tentative smile. "So am I." She glanced between the two women and asked, "I didn't think you started for another two weeks. Is today your first day?"

She shook her head, her curly light brown hair flicking over her shoulder. "Not today. I'm starting orientation on Thursday. Hannah and I moved it up."

Hannah added, "She said she's already settled into her apartment, so it made sense to get her oriented a few weeks earlier than we anticipated. So we'll start her on a Thursday through Sunday schedule until she's trained. Maybe for the next four weeks."

"Excellent." Tulsi forced a chipper attitude, though she was less than pleased. "If you'll excuse me, I have a client waiting for sign-out paperwork." She held up the handful of paper. Maybe Hannah noticed they were pre-printed care documents, but Frances apparently didn't.

"Sure thing," The perky green-eyed young woman said, stepping aside so Tulsi had room to pass in the hallway.

Fleeing the scene, Tulsi popped into the discharge area to give the owner the care directives and feeding information. That done, she peeped around the corner to see if either Hannah or Frances were in sight. They were.

Down by the break room, Hannah and Frances stood in the doorway. A small crowd of vet techs and clinic staff smiled and shook hands with the new veterinarian.

Gall rose in Tulsi's throat along with her blood pressure. What was it about the witch that always had everyone accepting her so readily? Tulsi compared her own first introduction to the clinic employees five weeks ago. She had shown up in scrubs with her usual no-makeup look. They had been standoffish. No handshaking, no laughing and answering questions as Frances was now doing down the hall. The cold shoulder of the office staff hadn't thawed yet despite her being there more than a month already.

Sooner or later, they might feel differently. At Cornell, Frances had been sweet enough at first to everyone, but she had shown her true colors over their four years together. She was an extraordinary gossip. Nothing escaped her notice nor her opinion or comment. If she didn't *know* what happened, she'd speculate. Usually the guess became a false truth and part of the revolving gossip. Whoever she picked to slander didn't have a chance at getting the real story out. Frances's version was more salacious than the truth, which made it such a good story to share and made the nonfactual version impossible to kill.

Tulsi had been a frequent victim of Frances's gossip. Her innuendos and assumptions had everyone in their class thinking Tulsi was the by-product of her mother's rape by an Indian felon. Few gave Tulsi the chance to correct the story. Hannah and Cortland did and quickly became Tulsi's friends.

Over the four years, no one was spared the lashing of Frances's gossip. Her former acceptance became notoriety until Frances was without a single friend by the end of the program. *Served her right to be alienated like that after her malicious, wagging tongue.*

Tulsi hoped the woman had learned how to curb her imagination and her tongue in the two years since graduation. Otherwise, she wasn't going to last here at the clinic. Hannah had made it exceptionally clear during her Zoom interview that such gossip would not be tolerated. Hannah and Cortland had been hurt by Frances's exploits, too. When they had revealed Frances was joining the clinic, Tulsi couldn't believe it. Frances's grades and skills had been passable, not stellar. Hannah had explained she couldn't dally with the hiring as Cortland was leaving for Alaska as soon as she could. So she hired knowing what she would get rather than take a chance on someone she didn't know.

Hannah warned Frances she would be on probation for eight months. If any trouble arose, she'd be out on the street. Tulsi and Cortland had a bet on how long Frances would last before being fired. Tulsi guessed three months, Cortland bet on five. Hannah wanted to join the bet but since she would be the one deciding about any firing, she recused herself.

CHAPTER FOURTEEN

The Irish Harp was unusually noisy Friday night. It was bursting at the seams with off-duty firefighters by the time Lucas arrived. Fast, Celtic music played by a small band on a dais added to the overly loud atmosphere. The aroma of burgers, onion rings, hot wings, and whiskey lingered in the air, making Lucas's mouth water. He pushed his way up to the guest of honor at tonight's celebration. Dawson sat on a stool beside the ornately carved bar, talking with a few guys from Station Three. When he saw Lucas approaching, he stood. Grasping his former firefighter around the shoulders, he drew Lucas in for a manly hug and a slap on the back. "Luc, I'm glad you made it."

"Wouldn't miss saying goodbye for anything except a five-alarm job," Lucas chuckled and took the bar stool vacated by someone else.

"I heard you passed both tests, and the selection committee thought your interview went real well."

"I still didn't get it." Lucas see-sawed his head. "They had great fun teasing me about my truck, though."

Dawson shrugged. "I'm sure you expected that going in."

"I was hoping they wouldn't mention it." He scrubbed his jaw before continuing. "Anyway. They noted my knowledge of the town, like you suggested. They reviewed some of the jobs I'd been on during my two years. It felt like it was going good." He sighed and shrugged.

Dawson pointed his finger. "Don't forget what I told you. When my position's filled, another lieutenant's position will open." He poked his finger into Lucas's chest as he spoke, "Do not forget to apply for it. You're sure to get it."

Lucas snatched at Dawson's finger but missed. He saluted instead. "Aye, aye, Captain." He gave this man, his mentor in the fire department, a handshake. "I'm going to miss you, Dawson. You've been inspirational."

Leaning forward to get close to Lucas's ear, Dawson whispered, "Don't tell anyone, but I changed my mind about Ohio."

Lucas's spirits surged as he couldn't believe his ears. "So you're staying?"

Dawson shook his head and said, "I'm looking for a job in Alaska. Somewhere close to Cortland's place in Hope."

His eyebrows rose in surprise. As Dawson's words sank in, a grin grew on his face. "I see."

"Don't tell Tulsi or Hannah. I want to surprise Cortland. If she'll have me." He gave Lucas a wink.

Dawson pulled him in for another hug. "Take good care of Tulsi. She's something special."

"Don't I know it." Lucas winked back before moving up to the bar for a Harp lager.

Speaking of Tulsi, Luas realized he needed to call her. Pulling out his phone he tapped her name on his screen. When she answered, he said, "Hey, sweetie. How's it going?"

"It's tense. The new vet arrived early and started yesterday."

An odd mixture of relief and disappointment swirled in his gut. "I have to work two doubles, Saturday and Sunday. I'm sorry I won't be able to see you."

"Me too. It's just as well. Both Hannah and I will to working all weekend with Frances in training."

He could hear the disappointment in her voice, and perhaps a little frustration. "Everything going okay?"

"Uh, sorta," Tulsi replied. "It's just that, well, the staff seem to be agog with Frances." She sighed heavily. "I can't explain it very well. In only one day, she seems to have slipped into her position like a warm knife through butter, if you can excuse the cliché."

Aware of how alienated Tulsi felt with most of the clinic staff, he understood the subtext of her words. "Don't worry. It might take some time, but I'm sure you'll all become a cohesive clinic family again." He knew how patronizing that statement sounded but he couldn't think of anything else to say over the phone that might give Tulsi some comfort.

With a doubtful tone of voice, Tulsi said, "Yeah, right."

CHAPTER FIFTEEN

Monday morning, Tulsi's anxiety was back under control. She was grateful that Frances had the day off so she and Hannah could return to their smooth working groove.

It had been a harrowing weekend at the clinic with Hannah and Frances. Between the usual parade of clients and their pets, Hannah had been seeing her patients with Frances as her assistant. Tulsi knew Hannah wasn't a fan of Frances, but seeing them working side by side like conjoined twins had infuriated her. She tried to remind herself Hannah had done the same with her, while Cortland handled the rest of the workload, but this felt different. The three of them were tight friends, while Hannah, Frances and she were not.

At lunch in the break room on Monday, Tulsi listened to the excited chatter of the staff over the new arrival. Their voices swirled around and past her like she wasn't sitting there.

Valerie praised the new trick Frances had explained about injecting vaccine in a feral cat through the soft-sided carrier. Clarissa said Frances asked her to take her to all the hot hook-up sites in Colby, and she would pay the way. Megan said she was so friendly to that mean old Mr. Crowe he left with a smile. She was pretty, her shoes were top-notch, and even her scrub clothes were the height of scrub fashion.

"Ugh," Tulsi said, getting up from her chair. "I forgot to order my brother's present online." Nobody noticed or seemed to hear her. It was like she was invisible.

She paced her office, peeved at the immediate acceptance Frances had received from the staff. Yes, Frances had been outwardly friendly, just like at vet school. Tulsi had been more reserved. It was a by-product of her upbringing. Her skin color put most people off. She was deemed different. A foreigner despite being a US citizen. Their reactions made her shyer, more timid, helping to form her introverted personality.

Looking different in such a small town as Chilton was enough to make her feel like an outsider.

Would they like her as well if the gossipmonger started up? Tulsi prayed that Frances had learned her lesson by now. Only time would tell the truth.

Later that night, Tulsi sat cross-legged on the couch in her pajamas, eating a bowl of cereal while watching a reality TV show about a veterinarian in Alaska. It reminded her of Cortland and her new gig as a part-time vet at some wildlife sanctuary in Girdwood. The reruns were as good as the first time she saw the episodes. After a long day at work, she should be watching something completely unrelated to her job. But she watched, hoping the episodes might give her tips for dealing with the staff and clients at the clinic.

Maybe it would give her some insight into why her coworkers weren't as welcoming to her as they were to Frances Mueller.

Tulsi didn't want to believe the reason she suspected. The skin color issue manifested at her first real job in Louisiana. Surely Connecticut would be far more open to people of another race? Yet, it didn't feel like it from her perspective. The staff shared jokes and long discussions with Frances and Hannah but not with her.

Why am I always on the outside, wishing to get in? Or why can't I learn to be happy being solitary?

Her phone rang. She muted the television.

"Hey, it's me," Lucas said. "Sorry I haven't called. I was on double twenty-four-hour shifts this weekend, and it was biz-ee. I've been anxious to call you."

"That's okay. Hannah, Frances, and I were busy all weekend, too." He'd never left her thoughts since they last talked. All along she wished Frances would be starting earlier than August first. She groaned, thinking she had got her wish and that she was regretting it already.

"Are you sitting down?" Lucas asked, his voice cracking.

TULSI'S FLAME

Was it a harbinger of not-so-great news? Tulsi set her bowl on the side table and steeled herself. A memory of Cortland getting a call that Dawson was hurt at a fire scene made her want to throw up. Sweat dampened her armpits and face as she waited. "Yeah. What happened?"

"I didn't get the promotion."

She let out a whoosh of breath, jumped up from the couch, and began pacing. *Thank you, God.* "Oh, Lucas. I'm so sorry." Her heart ached for him. It was something he really wanted. She could relate to the disappointment of not getting what you wanted.

His voice cracked. "I was second choice. The committee told me I should try again when another lieutenant's position comes available."

"How long will you have to wait?" She caught the images flickering across the television screen. The vet and staff were trying to examine a not-so-cooperative moose calf. It was one of her favorite scenes in the series.

"Not too long. Dawson's replacement is still being decided. It will likely be someone who's already a lieutenant. And that would open another position I'm able to apply for."

"Able to?" Tulsi asked. "Won't you go for it no matter what?"

He sighed. "I'd really like to stay with Station Two. The next opening might be for another station."

"Are the other stations so bad?" She sat down on the couch and paused the show.

"Station One isn't too bad. It's beside the department headquarters, so there's a lot of upper echelon around on a daily basis, which is good for getting noticed in a good way. Station Three is the opposite. I've heard lots of morale problems and procedural errors going on there. I don't think I'd like to transfer there, not even for a promotion."

She felt bad for him. He had wanted that promotion at Station Two badly. "Well, fingers crossed another opens up at Station One or Two."

He sighed again. "Don't worry. I'm not going to dwell on it. It isn't my time yet."

"What are you doing tonight?" she asked, picking up her cereal bowl again. "Want to come over?"

"Wish I could. I'm with some firefighters at the pitching booth in Wilkesbury. There's an upcoming charity baseball game between Colby's fire department and the police department."

"Oh." Tulsi hadn't known anything about it. Probably because she was so new to town.

"Anyway, besides sharing the bad news, I want to ask if you'll go to my niece's quinceañera with me. It's on Saturday."

"What's that? I've never heard of it." She put him on speaker and started checking her calendar.

"It's a common celebration for us, Boricua. It marks a girl's passage into womanhood on her fifteenth birthday. It's part social and part religious event."

"What's the appropriate attire?"

"Modest, Sunday kind of attire. The first part of the ceremony takes place at Our Lady of Divine Providence Catholic church. Afterward, we have a reception, much like a wedding reception." He offered, "I'll be wearing a suit."

"How about a gift? Should I bring a gift?"

"She has a gift registry. A small iTunes gift card would suffice."

Tulsi picked at her cuticles. Was it a good idea to accept his invitation? She remembered the evil eye his mother had laid on her. "What about your family? Your mother especially. She didn't like me the only time we've met. Remember?"

"Hmm. True. But my mom was overreacting because of her dinner party. The one I skipped out on. She was angrier with me than you."

She wasn't sure she believed him after what he'd told her earlier. That his mother was anxious because he was interested in dating someone who wasn't Puerto Rican. Tulsi remained silent as she mulled over the options.

"Come on. It's a fun event. If you've never been to one, it's a great opportunity to learn about a small portion of my culture."

"You want me to learn about your culture?" she asked, feeling goosebumps at being invited now. Was Lucas suggesting she should get familiar with his culture? Was he saying they might have a future together?

"Of course I do. It will help my mother accept you. My entire family, too."

She raised her eyes to the ceiling and closed them. This may end up being a nightmare, but she did want to make a better impression on his family. Steeling herself, she gnawed on her knuckle before blurting out, "Okay. Hannah and Frances are on duty that Saturday. I'll go."

"Great, I'm so excited to introduce you to the whole family." Lucas's voice was exuberant, exploding with excitement. "Can we meet at the soccer fields tomorrow night, about nine pm? There's a meteor shower happening, and the skies should be clear."

A warmth spread through her chest. Lucas paid attention to the things she loved to do. And he wanted to participate in that activity with her. "That sounds like a great idea. I think it's a quarter waxing gibbous moon, so the moonlight might interfere, but I'm game if you are."

"I'm always game with you." His voice was soft this time, warm enough to make her heart beat faster.

CHAPTER SIXTEEN

After work the next day, Tulsi swung home to change and eat dinner. It was their last day working together before Frances came back. While it was not hot, it wasn't exactly cool either. Throwing on a light, long-sleeved top and her favorite jeans, she headed out the door.

Tulsi met Lucas at the soccer fields as they had planned. He stood beside the loaner vehicle that definitely didn't fit his personality, decked out in tight jeans. They outlined his muscular thighs and lower legs, which she knew were lightly fringed with fine, light brown hair. A shiver went down her spine, remembering the feel of those legs sliding down her own bare legs, tangling and caressing as they snuggled and rolled around her bed.

He reached into the open driver's window and pulled out something about a foot long and high. "I bought you a present," he said, thrusting the box toward her. "I thought you needed a pet."

Tulsi held the box up so she could see inside through the small airholes in the cardboard. "What is it?"

"A leopard gecko. I have a tank, food, and accessories for him, too. The guy at the pet store said they're popular and easy to care for." His face got a serious look as he added, "I hope he didn't steer me wrong."

That warmth returned as she saw the little gecko hanging out in the box. "He was right. It's a popular reptile and easily managed. Thank you." She leaned over, meaning to give Lucas a quick kiss on the lips, but his arm wound around her waist and pulled her in closer for another lip-smacking long kiss that made her toes curl and her lady parts warm.

"Let me put him in my car." Together, they placed the items and the gecko in her car and grabbed her binoculars and her sky chart before returning. "Shall we?"

Lucas hung his head. "I forgot to bring binoculars. Actually, I'm not sure where they might have gone. It's possible my brother Juan confiscated them when he moved out."

She bumped her arm into his as they walked to the center of the field. "No problem, I can share."

Tulsi oriented herself to the night sky, figuring out north from south. Lucas flicked on his cellphone's flashlight so she could examine the chart and see what they might be able to spot in the darkness above them.

"So, I think Vega is that bright star right there." Her arm pointed up into the eastern sky. "It's the fifth brightest star in the heavens and the first star to ever be photographed back in the mid-1800s. It's in the constellation Lyra."

"Huh." Lucas craned his head back to look overhead. "It's a little hard to see with the moonlight," he paused before adding, "okay, I see it."

Tulsi scanned the sky, looking for something. "Yeah, the moonlight is interfering a bit. We can still find other great things to look at." They were both silent a moment before she said, "Ah ha! There it is!"

"What? Saturn?" Lucas said, his face raised toward the night sky, scanning.

"Not Saturn, though with binoculars, you can see the rings in the winter. You can see Jupiter now." She handed them to him and gave him verbal directions on where to look for the planet.

Lucas searched, his eyes scanning the heavens with the binoculars. "I don't...wait...I found it! Wow, that's amazing! I didn't know you could see planets with only binoculars!"

They were shoulder to shoulder, Tulsi looking at him while he observed the sky. "There's a lot we can see without binoculars."

He lowered the instrument and turned to her. "You're more amazing than the stars." He kissed her soundly as they clung together.

When they broke apart, Lucas said, "I almost forgot. I have a blanket in the car. Let me get it, and we can lie back and enjoy the view."

He did as suggested, returning with the picnic blanket and laying it out before Tulsi. She spread out on it, face up, and Lucas joined her. Her hand reached for his after he was settled. He grasped it and brought it to his lips for a kiss before lowering it but stayed connected to her.

They viewed the sky, chatting softly. Tulsi pointing out various constellations as she recognized them. Lucas following, trying to see what she was seeing. A few shooting stars wizzed by, giving them both an opportunity to make a wish.

Eventually, she was silent and turned on her side to face him. Lucas turned too, leaving less than a foot a space between them. He brought her hand to his lips again, but this time, he let his tongue search out the nooks and crannies between her fingers.

"That tickles." Tulsi giggled before searching out his lips with her own. She sighed audibly at their softness and when Lucas shifted into kissing with abandon, Tulsi went with him.

In seconds, they lay naked in each other's arms, making love so slowly Tulsi forgot the time, the stars, and everything else. After they both reached climax, they lay back, panting with the effort, not speaking until Tulsi broke the silence, "I think I have a thousand mosquito bites." And despite the irritation in her comment, she started laughing. "We should have brought some bug spray or at least a citronella candle."

"Let me kiss them." Lucas pulled her in his arms again and started kissing her all over until she stopped him.

She clutched his head, holding it still. "Stop. We should get going."

He reluctantly agreed, and they dressed, picked up all their paraphernalia, and returned to their vehicles.

"Do you want to come over?" Tulsi asked, leaning against her car.

TULSI'S FLAME

Lucas stood directly in front of her. "I'm afraid I have to be in for the morning shift tomorrow. One of the guys has a medical appointment, and I'm covering until he gets back." He leaned in to kiss her. "I'll take a rain check." He kissed her again, longer and more sensually this time. She heard the rapid thud of his heartbeat that matched her own. "I'll be busy all Thursday and Friday trying to help my brother paint the house."

"That's a big job." Tulsi kissed him back, letting her lips linger on his.

"No kidding. But it has to be done before Saturday, for the gathering at the house after the quinceañera party. It'll be hot, but we'll get it done. Marco and my brother, Juan, will be helping, too."

Tulsi nodded. "So I'll see you on Saturday? By the way, I'm paying for everything."

"No, you're not. I asked you. You are my plus one." He squeezed her hand. "I'll pick you up about eleven in the morning."

CHAPTER SEVENTEEN

Tulsi gasped and stumbled backward when she opened the door on Saturday.

Lucas stood there with a broad smile on his face. "I clean up nice, don't I?" He held up his hands before twirling around so she could inspect his attire. "Well?" he demanded, swaggering into the condo.

Tulsi raised her eyebrows. "This suit is sexier than the one you wore at the wedding. Where did you get that outfit?" Her hand waved in the air as she gave him a piercing glance up and down.

The cut of his suit was exquisite, and the navy pinstriped fabric showed off his trim physique without clinging too tightly to his body. It clearly outlined his muscular thighs, his broad chest, and the contours of his shoulders and upper arms. The gleaming white of his shirt radiated through the open vee of the jacket. "I had it made in San Juan last time I visited my tios."

"Tios? Family?" She approached him, one hand on her hips, exaggerating their sway. Her arm slipped around his waist as she licked her lips.

His eyes watched her tongue. "Yes, my uncles and aunties. Some are going to be there today. In fact, a bunch of them have arrived at the house, creating a lot of noise and parking all over the road. I'm sure the neighbors will be complaining again," he said as he pulled her against his torso. "Where's my hello kiss?" he asked softly before his lips joined hers.

Her mouth opened and he accepted the invitation, teasing his tongue over hers, biting her lower lip before sucking on it. She returned the favor eagerly, wanting to stay in his arms for the rest of the day.

He stepped away from her. "If we don't stop now, we might not make it to the church on time. My mother would never forgive me." He looked her up and down appreciatively, a hunger still shining in his eyes. His smile melted into a frown, taking on an uneasiness she had never seen before. "Is that the outfit you're wearing?"

Tulsi's stomach dropped as a clamp ringed around her throat. "Yes. Why?" She had no idea why his expression had changed so precipitously. "What's wrong with it?"

Lucas scrubbed his hands together, interlaced his fingers, and cracked his knuckles, his facial expression still tense. "It's just that," he paused and wrinkled his nose before replying, "the court has the same color scheme as your dress." He stopped as though thinking whether to say anything else but added, "And our church doesn't like bare shoulders on a woman. It's considered disrespectful."

She blinked, trying not to cry. Didn't it figure that no matter how hard she tried to fit in, there was always something that set the rest of the people against her. Tulsi had no idea what color the court would be wearing. Nor did she know anything about Lucas's church's prohibition on bare shoulders. Her wardrobe didn't have many nice, church-style clothes. This outfit, a bright sunny yellow wraparound sleeveless dress, was her best. "I..." She sighed heavily. "I'll go see if there's something else I can wear." Escaping to the bedroom gave her a few minutes to wipe away the tears threatening to slide down her cheeks. Tulsi peered into the closet, going through her limited fashions one by one. The hangers tangled, scrub shirts fell off their hangers to the floor. Anger flashed through her, white, hot, and boiling in a rage she hadn't felt since before she left her job in Louisianna.

She jerked away when Lucas's hand touched her shoulder. "Don't. Please," she cried, trying to tamp down her feelings so as not to explode at Lucas. He didn't deserve it, but she wished he had told her what shouldn't be worn and why.

He wrapped his arms around her shoulders, pulling her against him. Her head fell to his collar bone, and she held on as though her life depended on it. "I'll help you find something a little more...acceptable."

She clung to him, trying not to get tear and snot stains all over his beautifully cut suit jacket. "I—I don't have much. Most of my clothes are for work: scrubs, jeans, tee shirts, and casual tops." She broke free from his embrace and wiped her eyes. "This dress...it's the only one I have. I wore it to graduation from vet school."

"Let me have a look." Lucas scrolled through the hangers, pausing a few times to contemplate an outfit. When he got to the end, his face was as miserable as she felt. "Okay. I didn't see anything. But this shawl can cover your shoulders in church." He held out the ivory-colored shawl. Tulsi took it. She could see he was thinking hard, the gears in his brain working overtime to figure out a solution. "Maybe Hannah has something you could wear? We'll be late, but it's better than..." He let the last of his sentence slide.

Tulsi's chest felt hollow. "Hannah's working. I can't ask her to leave the vet clinic on a Saturday to find me a dress."

Lucas mashed his lips. "Well then, we go as we are. How bad can it be?"

CHAPTER EIGHTEEN

Truth be told, it was bad. Tulsi had grabbed a black sweater to bring with her, but Lucas had nixed that as well. "Black is the color of death. We don't wear black to happy events." She ended up taking the shawl with her when they arrived at the church.

The ceremony had already started when they entered. The vestibule was small and old with ornate woodwork crafted decades ago by parishioners. Lucas snatched a pamphlet for the ceremony off the tiny table at the entrance to the nave and handed it to Tulsi. Trying to be inconspicuous, they sat in the last pew, closest to the door. The clack of Tulsi's heels on the terra cotta tiled floor had more than a few heads turning. Among them, Lucas's mother glared an evil eye at the two of them, all the way from the front pew.

Most faces held hard stares, a few nods and smiles, directed at Lucas, no doubt. Overall, a chilly reception in the midst of the ceremony.

The priest, standing in the chancel, continued the ceremony. Tulsi was having a hard time understanding what he was saying. "Is he speaking English?" Tulsi whispered in Lucas's ear, to which Lucas shook his head before whispering back, "Spanish." She glanced at the pamphlet in her hands. It was entirely in Spanish.

Didn't it figure? Tulsi closed her eyes and tried to steel herself for a long night of ostracism with everyone speaking Spanish except her. That would mean few people might actually talk to her, ignoring her as though she didn't exist. If that was how the night would progress, so be it. Tulsi would keep a stiff upper lip until Lucas took her home. Or maybe if it got too miserable, she'd call an Uber and slip out of the reception hall when no one was looking.

She looked at Lucas. He was so intent on the proceedings, he paid her little attention. The church was beautiful inside. The twelve stained glass windows gleamed sunrays of color onto the far walls. The wood pews were not comfortable, but they probably were designed that way to keep parishioners awake during services. The chancel had a gorgeous apse. The ceiling was painted to show a large white dove, symbolic of the Holy Spirit, flying overhead. The upper margins of the walls in the apse held the words: "Ergo Sum Via, Veritas et Vita." She didn't need to know Latin to figure it meant, "I am the truth and the life."

The priest droned on and she went back to wallowing in her pity. Lucas poked her upper arm to get her attention and pointed at the altar. "My parents, as her grandparents, are going to give Anita her bouquet of fifteen roses."

When Tulsi gave a slight nod, he added an explanation. "One rose for each of her fifteen birthdays. The stems signify strength, and the petals of the roses signify sweetness."

As Tulsi watched, Mrs. Campbell, wearing a soft light green dress, and the man wearing a navy blue suit, approached the chancel where a young girl in a white ball gown stood before the priest. The man, she assumed it was Mr. Campbell, carried a bouquet of roses. Together, Mr. and Mrs. Campbell presented the roses to Anita. Lucas nodded his head in appreciation of the moment.

She had no clue what to say or do. It was all so foreign to her. Sitting through the remainder of the ceremony, she thought how it was funny that Lucas and his family came to the US and brought their culture with them. And even though Anita was born and raised entirely in the US, she was showing reverence and respect for the family's culture. Something Tulsi could never do for her own.

Saddened by the thought, she thought of her adoptive parents' attempts to expose her to Indian culture. Throughout her life, her parents took her to Indian restaurants so she could taste the samosas, curries, Vindaloos, and all facets of the food. They especially went on nights when someone was playing sitar music, so she might hear the sounds of her ancestral culture. At one point, her parents were considering taking her on a trip to India. It made no sense to her, and she'd nipped that idea in the bud.

She wasn't Indian. Not really, and she didn't want to be. Her biological parents had given her up. They hadn't wanted her; consequently, she didn't want them, their ancestry, or their culture. She was an American, born and raised in the US of A. It was enough for her.

Despite feeling 100 percent American, she knew from years of experience that no one would regard her as such. With a glance, her outside, her skin betrayed her inner core. To everyone else, she didn't fit in, and she never would.

The music struck up as Anita and her attendant proceeded down the aisle, trailed by the fourteen women and men. All the women wore yellow ball gowns, while Anita wore white. The young men wore dark suits with yellow bowties. As Anita approached them, she waved furiously at Lucas and blew him a kiss. Directly behind her were her parents, Lucas's sister Maria, and her husband, Benito Santiago, followed by Lucas's parents. Mr. Campbell shook his son's hand in passing and smiled broadly at Tulsi. Mrs. Campbell, however, scowled as she approached. For a fleeting moment, Tulsi thought she would stop and berate her son right there in the church. Fortunately, Mr. Campbell noticed her slowing pace. He tugged at her arm, snug in the crook of his elbow, and whispered something to her. She glared at her husband and then at Lucas and Tulsi but kept going.

Tulsi leaned into Lucas. "Is there a back door to this church? I don't want to get accosted on the front steps."

A worried look in his eyes, he nodded. "Yeah, let's go out the side door up near the altar. My mother doesn't look too pleased, and I don't want her to start anything that might ruin Anita's special day."

She and Lucas waited for everyone else to walk past before leaving through the side door and heading to his car. Tulsi trembled slightly as they got in—her head swiveling to look out for trouble in a pint-sized

Puerto Rican mama. Slamming the doors shut, Lucas locked them from the inside, revved the engine, and they took off for the reception.

The entire ride, Tulsi wanted to plead with Lucas to pull over and let her out on the sidewalk...any sidewalk. She didn't want to have an altercation with his mother or anyone else in the family. If that meant she bailed on the rest of the event, so be it. It certainly wouldn't be the first time she'd slipped out of something because of inhospitable looks, and she knew it wouldn't be the last.

CHAPTER NINETEEN

Lucas parked at the far end of the lot at the reception hall. They sat in the car, waiting for everyone to enter the hall before getting out.

"Do you think it's safe?" she asked, deep lines between her eyebrows. "Maybe we shouldn't go. Or maybe I shouldn't." Seeing the look of disappointment in his eyes, she added, "You go. You don't need me here. I'm sure my presence will make everyone uncomfortable."

Including me.

The light in his eyes flickered and dulled. "I really want to introduce you to my family." He grasped her hand and brought it to his lips, leaving a soft kiss on her knuckles. "I understand your fear. Backing down now would be a terrible thing to do."

Tulsi noted he said "backing down" rather than "backing out." Should they back down? Yield to the present wishes of his mother? Or back out of the commitment to attend the ceremony. Was there any difference between the two? "You think we should go in and your families' reaction be damned?"

He nodded briskly. "I do. Giving in to them would set a bad precedent." Seeing Tulsi didn't feel convinced, he added, "I've never interjected my feelings about anyone else's choice, good or bad. I refuse to let them do it to me."

It was a tough argument to disagree with. Lucas was an adult, as was she. He didn't need his family's permission to date anyone he deemed acceptable. She didn't either. "We'll have to be a strong front to withstand those who disapprove."

"We will," he said before placing his free hand on the door handle. "Ready to conquer the Lopez and Campbell families?"

She closed her eyes and sighed. "Ready as I'll ever be."

And with a click of the door latches, they made their offensive move.

As they opened the door to the hall, they realized their mistake.

Everyone else had entered and sat down. Everyone except Anita, her court of honor, and her parents and grandparents, all of them gathered in the foyer of the reception hall.

There was no way to gracefully slip by them as they waited for the announced entrance.

Lucas put his arm around her waist and propelled her forward. They skirted behind the cluster of young women in their sunshine yellow ball gowns. A yellow that perfectly matched Tulsi's dress. Clear of those waiting for the DJ to announce them, Lucas found their table assignment, and they hastened to sit down.

Settling into her seat, Tulsi scanned the hall. It was full of tables, each holding half a dozen or more attendees. Two front tables on a dais for Anita and her attendants, plus her parents and grandparents. Real flatware, abundant yellow floral centerpieces, and crystal adorned the table, the crystal sparkling in the light of the chandeliers illuminating the room.

Tulsi relaxed a little, seeing the pleasantly smiling faces around the table. Perhaps everything would work out well. She knew his mother would be over to visit the table where Lucas sat. It was only a matter of time. The likely confrontation made her stiffen her neck and grind her teeth. She would have to keep her eyes open to see Mrs. Campbell coming.

Before he sat down, Lucas introduced Tulsi to the other guests. "Hey—this is Doctor Tulsi Anthony." He went around the table clockwise from Tulsi's left to his right. "Here's Marisol, Juan's wife, and Juan. Next is Marco and his girlfriend, Lena. Beside Lena is my sister Arely and her husband, Sergio."

Tulsi's insides tightened. They were all Lucas's immediate family. Tulsi gave each of them what she hoped was a charming smile and a friendly hello in English. To her relief, none of them seemed upset meeting her. Considering how her children were all seated at the same table, Tulsi was sure Mrs. Campbell would be visiting.

Before she could breathe, a young boy ran over to Lucas and yelled, "Tio Luc, who's the cabecita you brought with you?"

Not knowing what the word meant, Tulsi kept the slight smile pasted on her face, her body frozen. The remaining adults scowled and called out, "Elian!" as Arely chastised her son for his manners. Lucas's face grew tense, the tic pulsing in his jaw expressing his displeasure with Elian's rude behavior. Arely's husband, Sergio, grasped his son's arm and led him away to a table with kids his own age.

The awkward moment was saved when the DJ began the sequence, announcing Anita and her escort, Victor, fourteen pairs of corte de honor participants, followed by her parents, Maria and Benito Santiago. Last to be announced were the grandparents. Benito's parents, Rosario and Orlando, and Maria's parents. Graham Campbell and Carmen Lopez strode in last and took their places at the head tables.

• • • •

Dinner was immediately served. It took some time. Lucas had told Tulsi that over one hundred and fifty relatives filled the hall. While they waited for their food, his stomach started to settle. His mother hadn't approached, probably due to his father's influence and his tight grip on her arm every time she tried to stand.

He decided to explain things about the event to Tulsi. "It's Anita's fifteenth birthday today, which is why it's called a quinceañera. There's fourteen young women, called damas, while the men are called chambelanes." He set his fork down, his plate empty. "After the dinner, there's a ceremony for the rite of passage."

Meanwhile, Lucas's siblings and their spouses were slipping her sly glances and whispering in Spanish among themselves between food courses. Tulsi's cheeks flared bright red. Lucas wanted to say something to his siblings, but it would be just as rude as they were. Since the conversation was in Spanish, at least Tulsi couldn't tell what they were saying.

"What does it entail?" Tulsi asked, her eyes sweeping the hall, watching the congregation of relatives as they ate, talked, and visited each other.

Before he could tell her more, the DJ started blasting music and introductions to the ceremony. Her chambelane, Victor, brought Anita to a chair in the middle of the dance floor. At this point, Lucas saw his siblings and their spouses get up from the table and cluster around tables with their children, leaving him and Tulsi all alone.

Tulsi's eyelids blinked several times as though she were trying desperately not to cry. His heart ached for her. Even though his siblings' desertion had been for logistical reasons, Tulsi took it as another abandonment by his family members. "They'll be back. They're all trying to get with their children, especially their daughters, to explain the ritual. Each will have her own quinceañera someday."

• • • •

Nodding her head as if she understood, Tulsi's mood sank. It felt like another snub. Would Lucas's family ever accept her? Teary-eyed, she watched Anita's parents, Maria and Benito Santiago, approach their daughter to start the ceremony. Her mother put lipstick on Anita's lips before settling a rhinestone tiara on the girl's head and securing it. Next, her father got down on one knee and slipped off her flat ballet shoes, replacing them with high heels. Lucas was whispering in her ear about the significance of each item. Each move was meant to symbolize her transition from a girl to a young woman.

Next, Mr. and Mrs. Campbell approached bearing a satin pillow. Lucas said, "The grandparents present her with a ring symbolizing the infinite circle of love from them." Anita's father's parents, Rosario and Orlando Santiago, did the same.

"I'll be right back," Lucas excused himself and advanced toward his niece, as did all his siblings, Antia's tias and tios. Together, they presented her with a teddy bear wearing a ball gown the same color as Anita's damas. Tulsi thought it strange that this ceremony thrusting Anita into adulthood would include a stuffed animal. The child's toy was incongruous with the theme of the ceremony.

When Lucas returned to her, she asked him about it.

"The presentation is called the ceremony of the last doll. Ceremonia de la última muñeca. The last doll which is dressed to represent her." He kissed Tulsi's cheek. "It's her last childhood toy. From now on, she will only deal with adult things."

She leaned over to ask Lucas something else as Anita's father, Benito, stepped up to the microphone with a glass of champagne in hand. Lucas translated the speech, "'Thank you all for being here to celebrate my little girl's transformation into womanhood. Please raise your glass, and with me, toast my daughter.'"

When a four-tiered cake was wheeled out, Tulsi was surprised again. It was like a wedding. Anita cut the cake, and everyone broke into song, a song in Spanish she didn't understand. Lucas joined in and explained afterward that they had sung the Spanish version of the Happy Birthday Song.

The DJ started a slow song, again in Spanish, as Anita and her father took the dance floor for a father-and-daughter dance.

When the song ended, the corte de honor assembled on the floor and performed a celebratory dance. It ended with the DJ cranking up the volume and starting fast-paced music.

Lucas grasped Tulsi's hand. "Come on, let's join the throng."

Sure enough, the dance floor became crowded with couples.

They danced to several songs, all wild and carefree. Everyone was dancing except for the older folk. Memories of their time at El Fuego filled her head. It was just like that night. Everyone dancing with wild abandon, flailing arms, turning, or spinning a partner. How no one injured someone else was remarkable.

When the dance music slowed, Lucas pulled her close. "How are you doing?"

Tulsi rested her chin on his shoulder. "Okay. It feels odd to not know what's going on, or what's being said. Is this almost over?" she asked.

"The dancing will continue until well after midnight. But we don't have to stay that long." Lucas raised his head unexpectedly. "My father is coming over to meet you."

Tulsi's knees weakened as a knot formed in her throat. Lucas released her, and his father took her into his arms to dance. Mr. Campbell said, "Halò lassie, Ciamar a tha thu? If you don't know Gaelic, that's hello, young lady, how are you?"

Tulsi stumbled, stepping on Mr. Campbell's toes. She hadn't expected him to speak in a Scottish brogue, especially not the Gaelic language, though Lucas had told her he was from Scotland. "Oh! I'm so sorry, Mr. Campbell," she exclaimed as a flush of heat raced across her face.

"No a bother," the man said in his thick Scottish brogue. "Call me Graham. You must be Tulsi."

She nodded and stammered, "Yes." She didn't know what else to do. Just then, Lucas and Mrs. Campbell waltzed past. Mrs. Campbell gave Tulsi the evil eye as she swept by in her son's arms.

"Dinae mind my wife. She's protective of her bebé. She'll come around sooner or later." He gave her a wink. "Besides, how can she bitch about Lucas's choice of a non-Puerto Rican spouse when she married a Scott, eh?"

The thought of the double standard and Mr. Campbell's mention of it made her laugh.

His eyes twinkled with merriment. "That's better. You should smile more. Don't let her or anyone else in the family frighten you. Lucas is sort of our golden boy. We're all protective of him."

Tulsi questioned why that was so but didn't ask. Why was Lucas so protected, more so than Marco, who she knew was the baby of the family? "What do you do? For work, I mean."

"I'm the regional safety manager for an airline. My territory covers all of New England. That's five large airports. It isn't many, but it's a lot of travel over six states. I'm not home often, and certainly not for long periods of time. There's always something happening."

The music transitioned to a fast tune before she could ask him more questions. He must have spied Lucas and his wife approaching. "I hope we have more opportunities to get to know you. Lucas looks smitten." He released her and stepped aside. Lucas traded places with his father.

Tulsi's shoulders dropped considerably, and she breathed a slow sigh as if releasing all the tension she had been holding during her dance with Mr. Campbell. When Lucas squeezed her tight to his chest, she leaned in and rested her head on his shoulder.

He looked at her expectantly. "What did you think of my father?"

She tried to pull together the right words to explain. When Lucas gave her a more quizzical look, she said, "He was nothing like I expected. He—was nice. And he seemed pleased to meet me."

He squeezed her closer. "I knew he was on our side. But I'm glad he told you."

Tulsi pulled back, scanned the room, and gave Lucas a hard look. "So one person in your family likes me. How many more do I have to win over? One hundred and forty-nine?" She raised an eyebrow, waiting for his response.

"One. The only other person you have to win over is my mother. When that happens, everyone else will fall into line."

She rolled her eyes. "Grrrreat," she drawled as she shook her head. "I'm going to the restroom."

CHAPTER TWENTY

Tulsi headed for the bathrooms outside the banquet hall. Mercifully, the room was silent as if unoccupied, except for the steady thump of the music. The mirror drew her. She leaned forward, wiping away the flood of tears with a paper towel before they could course down her face and smear her makeup.

From behind one of the partitions came a voice, "Can you believe he's more interested in that cabecita than Melena? Tulsi may be nice, but she could still be another gold digger looking for a sugar daddy like his last girlfriend."

The statement had Tulsi gripping the edge of the countertop. What to do? Tulsi decided she had nothing to lose as long as she got out of the restroom before the woman saw her and said, "I don't think she's a gold digger. She makes good money as a veterinarian." Tulsi paused. Should she try to get more information about his last girlfriend? What did she have to lose? "What happened with his last girlfriend? I can't remember her name."

"Sammy, short for Samantha. You would not believe. She invited him to move in with her. Within a week, she got fired from her job, or so she said and made Lucas pay for everything while she said she was looking for another. For nearly a year, the poor guy was paying her rent, utilities, food, gas for her car, getting her nails and hair done. Lucas was always broke. If she thought he had any money, she'd find a reason to spend it."

Tulsi's heart skipped a beat. She couldn't believe her ears and pushed for more information. "How did they break up? Did Lucas come to his senses?"

"Yes, he finally did. When she said she wanted her own credit card on his Amex account. He was smart enough to tell her no. She didn't like that and broke up with him."

"Thank God he finally had some sense," Tulsi replied, leaning back against the sink counter.

"No kidding! His brothers had been working on him, telling him someone who loved him wouldn't saddle him with so much debt. Anyway, he packed up his stuff and everything he bought her and moved back home. She begged and pleaded with him to stay, but he'd finally recognized her manipulations. Still, I'm not sure this new girlfriend is any better."

Tulsi's nerve endings all started firing, and her stomach went queasy. "Why do you say that?"

"He had to spend most of the ceremony translating and explaining what was happening."

Another voice answered back in a thick Spanish accent, "Si, she may be a veterinarian, but she's still an outsider. Her complexion is too dark. Why doesn't she stick with her own kind?"

The blood drained from Tulsi's face, and her throat clamped closed so tight she got dizzy and leaned over the sink, praying she wouldn't pass out. There were two women here! Heart pounding in double time, she heard toilet paper holders thudding as they were unrolled. Facing the women was not a viable option. She had to get out of there before they saw her. Two toilets flushing told her it was nearly too late.

She darted for the door. It opened from the other side. The woman blocking the doorway made her halt. Tulsi's knees shook as she reached for the wall to hold herself upright.

"Well, look who's here, girls," Mrs. Campbell said. "It's the puta."

The other two women chuckled behind Tulsi. Her eyes never left Mrs. Campbell's. She couldn't move. Her knees trembled under the cutting eyes of Lucas's mother.

"Haven't you anything to say?" Mrs. Campbell mocked. "Maybe we should call for help, girls. What do you think?"

Behind her, the two women cackled. "I think she needs to stay in her lane," one of them said.

Mrs. Campbell nodded. "Lucas needs to marry someone his own type. Someone who understands our cultural habits."

Tulsi flinched at the tight smile on Mrs. Campbell's face. She understood Lucas's mother was standing up for what she believed was best for her son. It wasn't necessarily meant as a microaggression. Still, her manner was aggressive. As they stood staring at each other, Tulsi gathered up her nerve, hoping to get away without making a scene or saying something she would regret. "I'm a veterinarian. I have no intention of hurting Lucas. I can take care of myself. I don't need a man to do it for me, and I never will. Especially not Lucas." When Mrs. Campbell didn't move out of her way, she said, "Please let me pass."

"Un momento," Mrs. Campbell said, holding up one index finger before shaking it. "You need to leave my son alone. Comprende?"

"S—si," Tulsi stuttered, her teeth clenched together so tight she couldn't speak correctly.

Mrs. Campbell crossed her arms over her chest. "Esta bien. Get out of here." She stepped aside, leaving space for Tulsi to flee.

She didn't hesitate.

Lucas was waiting outside the restroom door. "Are you okay? I saw my mother follow you..." He stopped speaking when he looked at her face. "What happened?" he demanded, his hands gripping her forearms.

Tulsi glanced over her shoulder, hoping Mrs. Campbell hadn't seen her son put his arm around her and steer her to the entrance of the building. She shook her head violently, her insides still taut, her brain still muddled.

"Are you okay? Did she say something to you?" Lucas demanded.

She shook her head again, not meeting his gaze. "It's fine. Everything's alright."

"Let's get out of here," Lucas said, not taking his eyes off her face.

When they got to her condo, he asked, "Can I stay? Do you want me to?"

She blinked rapidly. "Can I be alone for a few? You probably have to go home and change your clothes, right?"

He glanced down at his attire. "Yeah. I didn't remember to bring a change of clothes. Are you sure you're all right?"

"I'll be fine after a nap," she said, her palm clutched to her forehead.

He gave her a disbelieving look. "Okay. I'll be back later. Is that okay?"

She nodded. "Yeah, call me when you're on your way over."

CHAPTER TWENTY-ONE

Not long after Lucas left her, she got a call from Frances to come into the clinic. One of her regular patients needed help. Neither Frances nor Hannah was experienced enough with boa constrictors to deal with the issue. She changed her clothes and sped over to the clinic. An hour later, after settling the shedding issues with the snake, she walked out to her car. Lucas called as she got in. "I'm at work, I got pulled in for the overnight shift. But I wanted to tell you my parents' house was vandalized while we were at Anita's quinceañera."

His pronouncement stopped Tulsi in her tracks. "Oh my god. I can't believe it!"

"I can. The neighborhood punks have played games before. They've overstepped this time. The cops are investigating but, well, you know how it goes."

Tulsi's stomach dropped as she tried to fathom what Lucas had told her. "How?"

"The house was covered with spray-painted swear words, and things like, "go back to PR," and "get out of USA." All sides of the house and the roof were graffitied with racial slurs and threats."

"Oh my God, Lucas, was anyone hurt?"

"My mother nearly had a stroke she was so angry. We were able to calm her down, but it was a terrible thing to return to after Anita's celebration. Juan, Marco, and I are furious they did it over our newly re-painted house. Even the windows were marked up."

The thought that someone would do such a thing in Colby was unbelievable. How were the police ever going to catch the perpetrators? "Do you have a Ring doorbell or security cameras around the house?"

Lucas sighed heavily. "No. I tried to talk them into installing some kind of security system after the last attack back in January, but they declined." He sighed again. "I hope things are better in your end of town."

She scanned the entire parking area. Some of her coworkers were milling about, talking in small groups before going home. This was not the time or place to have a speakerphone conversation with Lucas about her confrontation with his mother. "Not really, but I don't want to discuss it now."

The fire alarm sounded loudly in the background. "Ugh, got to go. Call you later. Love ya, babe." The connection dropped.

Her breath caught in her throat at his last words. *Love ya, babe.* Was that true, or was it a slip-up? Or maybe he said that to everyone he cared for when he ended a phone call? Tulsi thought back over their previous calls. She'd have caught it if he'd said it earlier. She tamped down the flicker in her chest. It had to be a mistake. Didn't it?

Yet, his profession of love was like a lifeline, a life preserver to a drowning swimmer, buoying her up, giving her hope. Maybe he did love her despite his family's objections...especially his mother's.

She dropped her head in her hands and tried to shake the entire thing off. All her adult life, she'd looked at people's comments from every side, trying to determine if they were real or if there was some hidden meaning. A meaning that was demeaning. Here was Lucas saying something she was picking apart for truth or lie. With a deep breath, she decided to let the entire thing go. If Lucas really meant it, he'd say it again.

She clung to that thought as she drove home.

Several hours later, Lucas called again. "They found the culprits."

Tulsi instantly sat up alert. "Who? Who was it?"

"There was a group of seven kids, all from the neighborhood. The police checked the video doorbells up and down the street. A few neighbors had already erased their videos. But one hadn't. Several of the kids' faces were recognizable, and when hauled in for questioning, two of them spilled names. They're all being charged."

"So your family is pressing charges?" Tulsi wasn't sure that was such a great idea. It might enrage the families of those being charged and lead to more repercussions.

"They want the families to pay for cleaning up the mess and repainting the entire house. If the roofing shingles don't come clean, they want the entire roof replaced. It might cost tens of thousands of dollars with all that paint removal or coverup."

"I understand. That's not something they want to push off onto their home insurance policy."

"True enough." He paused a few seconds. "What are you doing tomorrow night? Any time for me?"

The bottom of her stomach fell. "No, sorry. I'm meeting up with Hannah for dinner. Afterward, we're going to Zoom with Cortland in Alaska at seven."

"Damn. I know you need your friends, but I'll be missing you."

How little he knew that statement was true. Except Hannah and Cortland were her only friends here besides him. "I'll miss you too. You and I can meet another night. Maybe?" She bit her lip, a flutter in her heart sending her pulse faster.

"Sign me up. When?"

"Dinner on Wednesday? Flora Café?" she suggested.

"That's the vegan place on Barker Avenue?" His words were hesitant.

From the tone of his voice, she noted he wasn't thrilled with the restaurant choice. "Yeah, or we can hit the Irish Harp."

"That's better. At least I can get some beer and a burger there."

Tulsi laughed. Lucas had no intentions of eating a vegetarian or vegan meal if he could help it. "I'm paying this time. No if, ands, or buts about it."

"But—" Lucas started.

"See you about seven," she said before swiftly disconnecting the call. It was no wonder Lucas's family thought she was a gold digger. He always wanted to pay for everything.

CHAPTER TWENTY-TWO

The need for coverage carried over through the day shift, giving Lucas more overtime. When a replacement finally showed up at three in the afternoon, he was out the door, ready for a shower and sleep.

His cell phone rang with a call from his brother Juan. "Lucas, are you on your way home?"

"I'm nearly there. What's up?"

"Can you swing by my house? I need an extra set of hands to help me with a plumbing issue."

"Is it the pool?"

"Something like that. I can't figure out what's wrong."

"Sure, I'm fifteen minutes out." Lucas groaned, then detoured toward Juan's house in Westerville. Turning onto the street, it was clear someone in the neighborhood was having a gathering. A dozen or so cars were parked at the end of the cul-de-sac.

Parking in the driveway of the small ranch house, Lucas walked around the side of the house along the palisade fence. A tantalizing aroma of roasting pork filled the air, making his mouth water and his stomach grumble. He'd left the fire station before dinner was served.

When he opened the gate door to get into the backyard, a chorus of "SURPRISE!" rang out in a few dozen different voices.

As everyone clapped along, they sang *Happy Birthday* in English before doing it in Spanish. "Cumpleaños feliz, tedeseamos a ti, cumpleaños a Lucas, compleaños feliz. ¡Felilz, Feliz en tu dia!"

Lucas grinned, his face flaming with heat. The crowd engulfed him in hugs, kisses, and backslaps as music started playing. His chest warmed with all the well wishes and congratulations on his thirtieth birthday. He'd known it was his birthday of course, but with everything else going on, he'd essentially forgotten about it.

Balloons and piñatas hung from the tree branches in the fenced yard. The kids, his nieces, nephews, and cousins played in the above-ground pool. Tables were laden with all sorts of summer foods. By the back fence, a whole pig turned on a mechanical spit, roasting over hot coals in a traditional trench. His stomach growled again, louder this time.

"You are hungry. Let me get you a plate of food," Tia Perla said before stomping off on her self-imposed mission.

Pulsing rhythmic salsa beats blasted the yard thanks to the mobile equipment courtesy of El Fuego's DJ. Marco, strutting to the music, sauntered over and shoved a Medalla Light beer into his hand. "You're going to need this," he said and quickly strode away.

In two seconds, Lucas understood why Marco did him that favor. His mother snuck up behind him, hugged herself to his side, and planted a kiss on his cheek. When she stepped aside, Melena Gomez stood behind her. "Lucas, you remember Melena."

The young girl blushed deeply as she said, "Felicidades."

The duckling, while not ugly, hadn't turned into a swan yet. Even if she were beautiful, she was much too young for him. "Gracias, Melena."

"Your mama has told me so much about you," Melena added, her blush deepening.

Lucas clenched his teeth behind his polite smile. His mother shouldn't have put either of them in this spot. "Wonderful." He glanced over her shoulder as if someone were summoning him. "If you'll excuse me, I need to talk to Pai." He stomped off to meet his father, ignoring his mother's calls to return.

Graham Campbell clasped his son's hand and pulled him in for a hug. "How are you?"

"Better now. I'm glad you're here. I thought you were going back to Logan Airport after Anita's quinceañera."

"I stayed a few extra days to celebrate your birthday." He leaned closer to his son's ear, "I couldn't tell you that, or I'd have been flogged." His father chuckled, and Lucas joined him, understanding the subtext.

TULSI'S FLAME

The warmth in Lucas's chest spread, knowing his father had extended his stay for his surprise birthday party. Many times throughout his childhood, his father had missed his birthday and that of his siblings. Perhaps he was regretting it now. Whatever it was that had Pai staying, Lucas was grateful.

Across the yard, the kids were squealing and calling out as one of his cousins batted at one of the piñatas. His eyes roamed the crowd, searching for his dark-haired beauty. "Where's Tulsi? Wasn't she invited?" His eyes narrowed at the thought.

"Nae." Mr. Campbell put his arm around Lucas's shoulder and steered him to a quiet spot. "Your mama wouldn't allow me to invite her when we were planning this party weeks ago. Your bràmair, Tulsi, should be here."

"And Mama pounced on the idea of making it a matchmaking event," Lucas said, swearing under his breath. "So Tulsi's not here. On my birthday, no less," he growled. Yet another matchmaking attempt by his mother. He shot his father a glare and stomped off.

He paced the yard, ignoring his father's calls, and fuming so hard, smoke should be pouring out his nose, eyes, and ears. The thought of calling Tulsi to come over went through his head. Yet he knew she was on duty at the clinic. It would not be kind to drop her into this den of vipers. Well, one viper and lots of pesky gnats.

He thought hard as he avoided anyone who tried to approach him. Seeing his mother heading his way again, her arm around Melena's waist, he decided enough was enough. Lucas walked back to his father. "If Tulsi isn't welcome here, I'm leaving." He hugged his father and kissed his cheek. "It's good to see you, Pai, but I've got to go."

His father's face showed his concern. He patted Lucas's shoulder. "I understand."

With his father's blessing, Lucas left his own birthday party.

CHAPTER TWENTY-THREE

Exiting the clinic exam room, Tulsi heard a loud ruckus coming from the break room. Hannah poked her head out of her office, a surprised look on her face. "What's going on?" she asked, glaring down the hallway. Mondays were always crazy, but this commotion was more than usual.

"I have no idea." Tulsi couldn't imagine what the uproar was about. On any given day, the clinic was quiet except for the sounds of their clients, barking dogs, howling cats, or the chirping of birds predominantly.

Hannah joined Tulsi to investigate the source of the chaos. Was it possible the entire staff was trying to capture an escaped client? It didn't happen often, but occasionally, an animal snuck out or bolted from its owner in the waiting room. Rarely did one manage to slip out of the exam rooms or from the holding kennels or post-operative recovery areas.

The two women glanced into the room from the doorway. All manner of excitement was going on. At the center of it stood their lead veterinary technologist, Valerie. Her left hand was extended, showing off a brilliant solitaire diamond ring for coworkers to admire, Frances among them.

"What happened?" Hannah said, a huge smile on her face as she approached the cluster of staff. "Valerie, you're not working today."

Valerie turned and held up her left hand. Her face brimming with excitement, her eyes sparkling as did the ring. "Craig proposed last night!"

Hannah gave the woman a huge hug. "That's so exciting. I'm so happy for both of you." Her face grew a little sterner when she added, "When's the big day?"

Valerie looked sheepishly at Hannah. "We're going to do a small service and a short reception on Saturday at the town hall."

"So soon? No big to-do for you?" she inquired. Modern brides typically wanted enormous weddings with all the expensive trappings, thanks to bridal marketing and magazines.

The bride-to-be shrugged. "We've been dating for years. Why wait longer and spend a ton of money on a one-day event?" She glanced at Hannah. "The boss here had the perfect idea of a small wedding and a low-key party afterward. We're thinking along the same line. Except we're ditching the church service for a civil one."

Hannah put her arm around Valerie's shoulders. "You will be a beautiful bride." She stepped away, giving Tulsi space to approach.

Realizing it was her turn to gush over the engagement, Tulsi stepped forward. While she was glad to see Valerie so happy, Tulsi didn't know the woman outside the clinic. Inside, she was levelheaded, competent, highly skilled at her career and her job. Tulsi wanted to convey her best wishes but felt restrained at showing her physically.

In the end, Tulsi took Valerie's hand and stared at the ring before looking up into Valerie's face. "It's beautiful. Congratulations." She smiled and stepped forward to give the woman a hug that wasn't quite a hug. Tulsi pressed her cheek to Valerie's but kept a lot of air between their bodies.

Valerie nodded, saying, "Thanks," before turning back to the crowd.

Barbra Pari poked her head in the door. "Sorry to break up the congratulations, but we have clients and their owners waiting in rooms two, four, and five."

"Oh dear," murmured Frances, heading for the door. "Where am I going?"

"You're in room five. Hannah is in room four and," she turned to look at Tulsi, "you're in room two."

The party broke up as everyone scattered back to their duty assignments for the day. Behind Tulsi, a small group of techs discussed bringing in food for a party on Tuesday to celebrate Valerie's engagement. She filed the announcement in the back of her brain, pledging to bring something spectacular for the party.

••••

Later that night, Lucas knocked on her condo door. He knew he was taking a chance even if her car was in the parking lot. She might be sound asleep all ready. When she opened the door, she was in her pajamas, her hair damp.

"Hey, is it okay for me to stop by?" He entwined his fingers and fidgeted with them. "I know we didn't make arrangements to see each other tonight." He tried not to stare at her breasts as her nipples hardened beneath the silky fabric.

Tulsi grasped his forearm and pulled him into the condo. "Not a problem as long as you're not asking me to go anywhere."

"How was your Zoom session with Cortland and Hannah tonight?"

Tulsi's nose scrunched. "We were supposed to, but it's been rescheduled. It's been a brutal day at work. Emotionally."

"Oh. I'm sorry," Lucas said with a grimace. "I'm glad you're here, though." Pleasure zipped through him for making an unexpected visit.

She stared at his face. "Oh no, what's wrong?"

"Is it that obvious?" He'd thought he'd done a better job hiding his emotions.

"Something happened and the displeasure is written all over your face." She led him to the couch and sat down facing him. "What's going on?"

Lucas rolled his eyes before closing them. "Long story short, my mother threw me a surprise birthday party yesterday."

Shock registered on her lovely face. "It's your birthday? How come you didn't tell me?" She leaned over and kissed him soundly.

He shrugged. "Frankly, I forgot about it with all the extra time at the fire station. Besides, I didn't want to make a fuss about it. Anyway, it was another one of my mother's attempts to introduce me to a girl she wants me to marry. Everyone in the family was there. Everyone except you. So I split, with my father's blessing."

"Are you serious? You left your own birthday party?" Tulsi shook her head, a look of disbelief on her face. "Why? Why not stay and enjoy being with your family?"

"You weren't there. My father said he'd asked to get you on the invitation list, but Mama nixed it in favor of Melena." Lucas pulled Tulsi close, his arms around her shoulders as he nuzzled her bare collarbone. "It wasn't a celebration without you. I would have stayed if you had been there. And I wanted to make it clear to my mother that I would not be manipulated. So, I left. I couldn't go home, so I bunked at the firehouse last night."

"But it was your birthday."

"It's not what I wanted. I'd rather spend my birthday with you."

Tulsi smiled and hugged him. "I don't know how old you are."

"Yesterday was my thirtieth."

"Mmm, an older man. I like that. I thought you were younger than me." She bumped her shoulder into his with a mischievous smile. "What should we do for your belated birthday celebration?"

His blood ran hot in his veins, and his cock stirred in his jeans. "I'm sure you can think of something."

• • • •

She beckoned him as he had beckoned her at the wedding reception, crooking her finger and shimmying down the hallway toward her bedroom, enticing him to follow.

Inside the bedroom, Lucas pulled her into a tight embrace. Her hardened nipples pressed into his chest as he kissed her with an intensity that had her entire body relaxing, surrendering to him. Fisting his shirt with both hands, their tongues danced a merengue. The alternating long and short probes sent shivers along her spine and warmth to her privates, awakening the need that had grown since their stargazing trip. The lingering taste of beer spurred her to search his lips, his tongue, his teeth for the malty, hoppiness he loved.

His hand slipped to her buttocks, kneading and caressing, setting match to tinder in her groin. Lucas pulled her against his pelvis. The feel of his cock, rigid against her pubic bone ignited her vagina with need. Something to clutch, something to fill her to the hilt. The aching need compelled her to grind against his tongue, his finger, and his cock until she came hard.

She broke their kiss and fumbled with his shirt buttons, her fingers trembling with unbridled desire. The anticipation became too much. "Fuck it," she said, her hands reaching to open his jeans. "I can't wait to feel you inside me, but it's *your* birthday."

"Mmm," he groaned, brushing her fingers aside to unzip his pants. Hearing the zipper fall, Tulsi dropped to her knees and sank her kiss-bruised lips around the glistening, wet head of his cock.

Lucas's hands tangled in her hair, holding her still as her tongue teased him, her lips still tight around his member. His loud moans accelerated her ministrations: licking the length of his cock while her hand caressed his balls, tightened and ready to spring. He pulled her away. "Stop, or I'm going to come now."

She smiled up at him, her eyes sparkling with mischievous intent. "What do you think I'm trying to do?" she said as her hand clenched his balls.

"You're sure?" Lucas groaned, leaning back.

Tulsi flicked her tongue out, reaching for his cock again. She watched him watching her as he inched his penis toward her outstretched, waiting tongue. Unable to resist, Tulsi pulled him closer to her mouth and licked the beads of moisture off the tip of his glans. The clenching of his balls told her he'd nearly lost it right then.

"Yes," he groaned as she engulfed his penis with her lips and milked him with her mouth.

He pumped into her soft, warm mouth, his hands holding her head steady. Once, twice, and on the third thrust, Lucas let the fire in his nuts spill. Tulsi placed her palm over his glans, letting the cum shoot into it. With that hand, she cupped his pulsing balls, as his thrusting slowed and the afterglow began. When he pulled back, she rubbed herself through her pajamas, feeling the ache in her swollen clit.

Reaching for her elbows, he raised her to her feet. "Your turn."

A thrill surged through her, knowing the ecstatic glow on his face was her doing.

Reaching out her hand, she stroked his cock back to rigidity. "I can't wait, give it to me, all of it." She kicked off her pajama bottoms and panties before leaning over the mattress.

"You got it, sweetie." Lucas stepped between her legs, spreading them apart with his knees, his hands clutching her buttocks.

Tulsi groaned. The emptiness of her groin demanded filling. His fingers slipped to her apex, making her tunnel slicker. A quivering started deep in her pussy. It wouldn't take long to detonate. "Please. Your cock," she begged. "Please."

"Wait a sec," he said, stepping back.

Lucas fumbled with his jeans and the condom before grasping her ass once more.. The smell of lubricated latex filled the room. "Now, please!" Tulsi breathed, her bottom wiggling with anticipation.

"I'm ready," Lucas grunted as the tip of his cock pressed gently against her folds. The wetness of the lubricant increased her urgency.

"Please," she moaned.

He pressed into her folds, separating them, the head of his cock sliding smoothly into the mouth of her vagina. "You are so fucking tight and wet, sweetie," He croaked. "Not gonna last long."

"Deeper. Lucas, please." Accepting her invitation, he stretched her opening and pushed in. The tightness, the fullness, had her crying out. "More!"

He thrust inside her to the hilt. Her pussy gripped his thick cock. She pressed back against it until the head rubbed against her cervix. "Fast, Lucas. Fuck me fast and hard!" she cried, and Lucas delivered. Slamming into her dripping wet pussy as he reached for her rock-hard clit. His fingertips found it and teased as his thrusting escalated beyond his control.

The explosion hit her as Lucas called out, "I'm going to come." They climaxed in an endless delirium of ecstasy before collapsing into each other's arms and resettling on the bed.

Lucas pulled the sides of the comforter over their spent bodies as they embraced face to face. "Best birthday present. Ever." He whispered into her ear before closing his eyes and joining her in slumber.

CHAPTER TWENTY-FOUR

Word spread quickly about the office celebration, and everyone brought something to eat Tuesday. The breakroom table was swamped with all kinds of things to eat, from chips and dip to finger sandwiches and at least ten different desserts. When Tulsi walked in, she was surprised to see Frances at the microwave. The odor coming from it was spicy. Tulsi saw one cleared spot on the table. She reached over to place her dish of cowboy cookies there, but a couple of techs said the space was for Frances's dish. The announcement raised Tulsi's blood pressure. Her eyes searched out another spot, only to find room on the counter beside the sink.

"Make way, ladies," Frances called out, hoisting her steaming plate above everyone's head. "Vegetarian samosas," she announced as she placed the plate in the empty table space. The heaping plate of golden brown triangles was immediately attacked from all sides. The moans of gastronomic pleasure filled the room as the samosas were devoured amid thanks to Frances for bringing them along.

Tulsi's interest was piqued. "Did you make those yourself, Frances?" The curt question came out without warning or design.

Frances and the others assembled glared at her. "No. They're too much work. Still, these frozen ones from the grocery store are good." She paused a second before adding, "Try one, tell me if you think it's authentic."

A few of the staff chuckled uneasily as Tulsi remained silent for a few seconds. "I wouldn't know if they are. I've never been to India. Besides, I hate Indian food."

"Weren't you born there?" one of the vet techs asked in an accusatory tone.

Tulsi shook her head. "No. Why'd you ask? Because my skin is a darker shade than yours?" She scoffed, "I was born in New Jersey.

I'm American." God, she hated, no—abhorred having to answer that question no matter where she went and who she socialized with.

Frances quipped, "Yes, of course," as if she didn't believe it. A few of the younger staff giggled at the take-down comment.

Everyone immediately dropped the subject when they saw Hannah entering the break room door. Hannah's face screwed up in disgust as she hastily pinched her nostrils, turned on her heels, and fled. Her reaction was so swift, so out of character, that everyone was astounded and began muttering.

It dawned on Tulsi immediately what had happened, and she followed Hannah to her office and made sure to shut the door behind them.

"Are you okay?" Tulsi found her friend seated at her desk, her head hung over the wastepaper basket. She ached to hug Hannah until she felt better, physically and emotionally. They hadn't discussed her pregnancy since Hannah told her about it weeks ago. She stood over her boss's crumpled form and gently rubbed her back as Hannah vomited. Neither said anything as Hannah's vomiting turned to dry heaves and finally subsided. Tulsi handed her a glass of water.

"Morning sickness?" Tulsi asked, picking up the trash can and sealing the contents in the plastic bag liner.

"Morning, afternoon, and night," Hannah gasped, wiping her mouth.

Tulsi pushed aside a pile of veterinary magazines and sat on the desk. "That sounds terrible. I'm sorry. Was it the smell that set you off?"

Hannah nodded, her face still pale and sweaty from heaving. "Everything sets it off. Even my morning yogurt. I had to stop eating it," her eyes got wide. "Guess what happened?" Not waiting for Tulsi to guess, she blurted, "Andrew hates yogurt, but guess what he's suddenly craving twenty-four/seven?"

"Yogurt?" Tulsi's hand covered her mouth as she tried not to chuckle at the situation. "I take it he knows."

"Yeah. He's over the moon. He wants to tell everyone, but I asked him to wait another month or so…just in case." Hannah shrugged. "It's still early. You never know."

Tulsi hugged Hannah. "I'm glad you told him, and me. When are you going to tell the staff?"

"I don't know. Andrew and I are going to the OB doc Friday afternoon. After that, we'll discuss it. I'd like to wait as long as I can, but I'm not sure I can tolerate the odors from the break room." Her eyes looked forlorn, pained. "I was thinking of asking them to keep the door shut at all times. Just in case." She shrugged. "I can't be leaving in the middle of an exam to run in here to throw up all day."

"True. Perhaps Barbra can put a sign up?"

"Yeah, good idea. I'll have to tell her why, but she can keep a secret."

"I'll go over now and shut the door. It sounds like the crowd has died down anyway."

She stopped by her office first. In the middle of changing her lab coat, she overheard Frances talking to someone outside her office door. She stepped closer to the door to hear what was being said.

"Do you want to know why Valerie and Craig need to marry so quickly?" Frances said quietly.

Megan's voice answered conspiratorially, "Yes. Tell me what's going on."

"She has to get married before she starts showing."

"OMG, are you saying she's, like, pregnant?" Megan's voice held a strong note of shock.

Frances swiftly replied, "Shh, don't tell anyone she's pregnant. Maybe Craig doesn't even know."

"Or maybe that's why he proposed?" Megan guessed.

"Well, like I said, don't say anything to anyone here."

Barbra Pari's voice echoed down the hallway. "Dr. Mueller, your patient has been waiting in room three."

"In a minute," Frances said. "I need to ask Hannah something first."

Tulsi's heart leaped for Valerie. She was the best vet tech to work with and the best of all they employed. She wasn't surprised that Frances had created this gossip. It was clear Frances had figured out Megan was the type to pass along the fake news. Hearing their retreating footsteps, Tulsi peeked out the door to assure herself the hallway was clear before heading for the break room.

• • • •

Frances approached Hannah's open door and knocked on the door frame. "Can I have a moment of your time?"

Hannah made no move to leave her office. "Yes, of course. What is it?"

"I saw the latest newsletter has a story on Tulsi and her 'special skills.'" Frances used her fingers to put air quotes around those words. "I was wondering if I can introduce myself in the next edition?"

The gesture irked Hannah, but she let it go. "I was going to have Barbra do it for you, but if you'd like to tackle that chore, be my guest. Keep it to less than one and a half pages. Can you get it to me by Friday? Barbra is already working on the next edition."

"Sure thing, Hannah." Frances's face broke into a wide smile before she walked away. Leaving Hannah with an uneasy feeling in her stomach that had nothing to do with her pregnancy.

• • • •

"Did you hear what Dr. Mueller told Megan a few minutes ago?" a voice, possibly Clarissa's, said from inside the breakroom.

Tulsi stepped back against the wall outside the door rather than enter the room. She didn't want to miss what was said.

"No. What did she say this time?" The voice sounded like Alissa Grainger, the office receptionist, but Tulsi couldn't be sure.

"She said it was suspicious they needed to get married so quickly. Dr. Mueller thinks Valerie's pregnant," Clarissa said.

"OMG, I heard someone barfing in the bathroom yesterday. I thought it was Dr. Woodbridge," Alissa replied. "Maybe it was Valerie. She doesn't look pregnant, though. And she's not exhibited signs of morning sickness. Not like Dr. Woodbridge."

Whoa! So Hannah's secret is out. Someone must have noticed how green she got before running off to the bathroom.

"Valerie has to get married quickly before she starts showing, according to Dr. Mueller."

"Where does that woman come up with such gossip? Last week she said that Dr. Anthony was screwing around with two guys at the fire department, playing one against the other."

Tulsi's jaws clenched. That little bitch was telling everyone she was having sex with two men? She stifled a growl as her stomach tightened in a knot over the accusation.

Both women giggled. "I don't know Dr. Anthony very well, but I can't see that happening, like, ever," Alissa said.

Her chest squeezed as she tried to figure out whether to laugh or cry over that statement. She did try to keep her personal life out of her work life. Maybe it made her too aloof. At least these women knew her well enough to understand the absurdity of Frances's gossip about her.

"Shouldn't we tell Valerie what Dr. Mueller is saying? Maybe she really is pregnant," Clarissa said.

"I don't know. I don't trust Dr. Mueller. She comes out with the strangest gossip. And she's not a very good vet. Her bedside manner sucks. Maybe we should wait for Valerie to hear from someone else?"

"Good idea," Clarissa replied.

Their voices got louder, as if the women were walking toward the door. "Maybe Dr. Mueller's intimidated?" Alissa asked.

"No, I don't think that's it. I'm guessing she doesn't have good people skills."

"Go figure," Allysa said with a laugh. "I'd expect that from Dr. Anthony, but she's great with clients. Dr. Mueller is chummy with us, so why is she so brisk with the owners?"

Fearing she'd get caught eavesdropping, Tulsi stepped away from the wall and acted as if she were walking down the hallway.

As she reached the doorway, she had to step aside to let Alissa and Clarissa exit the room. "Hi ladies, almost quitting time, eh?" she said, keeping her voice light and friendly.

"Sure is!" Megan replied while Allysa said, "Have a good night." Both women disappeared around the corner.

Tulsi entered the room. Everything had been cleaned up except her plate of cookies still sitting on the counter. She walked over and stared at it. Not a single cookie was missing. Her chest tightened, and her breath stilled at the obvious and intended slight.

Memories of grade school events where no one would eat the treats she brought. Memories of the birthday parties she wasn't invited to, and memories of the only time she had handed out invitations to her birthday party.

It was her seventh birthday. Her mother had made up a special, individualized invitation for each of her twenty-four classmates. Tulsi distributed them during recess, leaving the student's invitation on their desk. By the end of the school day, the trash can was full of them. Not one student attended. Not a single one.

Tears welled as she picked up the plate and dumped the cookies into the trash can before heading back to her office, shutting the door behind her. In her office bathroom, she turned the tap on full blast and gave herself a few minutes to cry out her anger and frustration before wiping her face with a cool cloth and moving on to finish her workday.

CHAPTER TWENTY-FIVE

Lucas called that night. At first, she wasn't going to answer. After leaving the office at six p.m., she'd gone straight home. Crumpled in a ball on the couch with a glass of wine and a tissue box by her side, she mulled over the day's miseries. Over and over again, she asked herself why didn't people like her? Was it entirely due to her dark skin?

Tulsi knew she wasn't the warm and fuzzy type. Her mother always told her she was outgoing as a child. It must have been the repeated rejections, the cold shoulders, and the invisibility she suffered that made her crawl into a shell. A shell that was hard to relinquish after all these years.

Until Hannah and Cortland came along. Her heart buoyed just thinking of how they had accepted her from the get-go. They had never questioned her about her birthplace or her parents. They understood and accepted her as she was...an introvert and a lonesome vet school student in need of a friend. To have these two young women accept her and encourage her through their four years at Cornell had been the saving grace of her early adult life.

When Hannah and Cortland first discussed getting an off-campus apartment together, they immediately asked Tulsi if she would like to join them. It had been the happiest time of her life. She knew their friendship had helped her blossom into a confident and highly skilled veterinarian.

And yet...here she was, letting the rejection of her coworkers get to her. Letting their snubs undermine her relevancy at the Colby County Veterinary Clinic.

On the fifth ring, she answered the phone. "Hey," she said, not knowing what else to say.

"Hey, you. What's going on? Why so glum sounding?"

Like liquid chocolate, his voice soothed her ears and her emotions. "Just a super bad day at work. I'll be okay by the morning." She knew it wasn't true. If she didn't have a day full of client appointments, she would call out sick. But her work ethic wouldn't let her. Like going to school, Tulsi would straighten her backbone and ignore their unfriendliness.

"Lose a patient, or was it something else?" Lucas asked, his tone telling her he was genuinely interested in helping.

"No, not veterinary related. Just..." she sighed heavily. "I'm finding it hard to fit in at work. No... make that fit in anywhere."

"Anywhere?"

Lucas didn't understand. Her voice hardened as she tried to convey all the things that kept her segregated from everything. "Like, at work, with my coworkers, my patients' owners..." she cupped her palm to her forehead to ease the headache she'd created with all her crying.

"I don't understand."

Tulsi stood and paced the living room. "Lucas, stop being so thick. You know exactly what I mean. We've talked about this before... About being left out, talked over, ignored like we're invisible."

"I don't feel that way now, and I don't understand why you do. Isn't Hannah treating you well?"

"No...I mean..." Tulsi cursed and scrubbed her hand over her face. "Lucas, it's not just my work. Hannah is treating me fine, but she's kinda distracted right now." She was silent a few seconds, "Lucas, your family doesn't like me. I've done nothing to them, and they dislike me. Your mother hates my guts,"

Lucas interrupted, "But my dad loves you already."

"Listen to me, please," she begged. "My coworkers treat me like I have the bird flu or rabies. They don't trust me and don't socialize with me. It makes for an uncomfortable and awkward day at the office." She flopped back down against the cushioned couch and slugged back the last of her wine.

He was silent. Or the line disconnected. "Lucas?"

He muttered something fast. So fast she didn't understand what he said. "What did you say?"

Louder and slower, he said, "I love you."

The shock of his statement had two entirely different effects on her. Her heart thudded harder and faster, warming her chest like a flannel blanket on a cold upstate New York winter night while her neurons froze to a solid lump, stilling her hands, her mouth, and her thoughts.

"Tulsi?" Lucas asked softly.

"Yeah?" she whispered.

"I love you."

"But—your mother, your family, they—" she sputtered.

"Only you matter to me. Even if it has to be just you and me, I'll be happy. So long as you're with me." He paused. "Look, I called to see if we can meet at the Harp on Friday?"

"Sure, what time?"

Their conversation was interrupted by the sound of a fire alarm. "Eight. Gotta go." Lucas ended the call.

He meant it. He really meant that he loved her. Her entire body tingled, all her nerves and neurons doing a happy dance. This was unlike the last time when he'd said "Love ya, babe." This time, the words were true and undeniably meant for her. Slumping onto the couch, Tulsi cried. This time, it was happy tears.

CHAPTER TWENTY-SIX

She returned to work the next day with a tightness in her shoulders and chest. Her head still ached from all the crying despite acetaminophen, eight hours of sleep, and three glasses of water to replenish her tears. By noon, she was feeling only slightly better. It was going to be one of those days.

During their collective lunch break, Tulsi stepped into the break room to get a spoon for her lunch. As she walked in, Valerie froze, and all conversation ceased. In Valerie's hand was a small stack of envelopes. A few of the staff held one, some open. The ache in Tulsi's forehead increased and spread through her core. Once she retrieved a spoon, she left the room but stopped outside the door.

"That was close," someone whispered.

Frances's voice called out, "You're not giving *her* one, are you?"

Valerie must have shaken her head because a collective sigh sounded along with a few murmurs of "thank God" and "Hallelujah."

It didn't take her long to understand Valerie was handing out wedding invitations. That familiar, socked-in-the-gut feeling filled her body. She wasn't getting one. She leaned against the wall, sighed heavily through her tight throat, and returned to her office.

Eating her black bean and corn salad, she fought back tears. It was status quo. She hadn't been invited to lots of events in her life because people didn't like her. They didn't want her around. Considered an outsider because of her darker skin color, even here, she was considered odd, eccentric, even warped for her love of caring for reptiles and other exotic creatures.

She wiped her tears away and flung her cup and spoon into the trash can as a light knock on her door sounded. Patting her hair in place with one hand while tossing all the used tissues into the waste basket, she called out, "Come in."

TULSI'S FLAME

Frances poked her head in Tulsi's office. "Can you cover for me this Saturday? There's an event I want to attend." A barely suppressed smirk played across her face.

Tulsi sighed, the hollowness in her belly getting larger. She didn't need to ask. It was the wedding. "Sure. But you'll be back on Sunday, right."

"Yes, of course. I'll be back Sunday, so you can have the day off."

With a curt nod, Tulsi cut their conversation short. Not that she thought Frances had anything of import to say. Given more time, she feared Frances would rub in the fact that she wasn't invited to the wedding. Faced with that distinct possibility, she abruptly said, "Frances, shut the door on your way out."

Frances gave her a smile that didn't reach her eyes. "Of course," she replied and shut the door behind her.

At the click of the door latch, Tulsi lowered her head into both hands, her elbows propped on the desktop. So that was the way it was going to be. Déjà vu of Louisianna. The same isolation and deliberate ostracism happened there with the staff.

It might be early August, but Tulsi was chilled. Hugging herself, she shuffled to her sole outside window, where the sun streamed through. The Town of Colby Animal Control van drove out of the parking lot. Knowing Hannah was probably free now that Andrew had left, she approached Hannah's office. She wanted to discuss this deliberate snub with Hannah but stopped outside her office door. It was unfair to burden her boss with this situation. Like she had done so many times before, she was going to have to suck it up.

Just as she turned to return to her office, she heard Barbra Pari's voice through the open door. "So you want me to ask Valerie to invite Tulsi to her wedding?"

"If you can. I realize Tulsi's still new here, but singling her out by not giving her an invitation is unacceptable."

Barbra said, "I understand. I hear they're talking about having a lunchtime bridal shower in the break room on Friday."

Hannah sighed. "Tell them to take it out of the clinic if they aren't inviting Tulsi. It's not fair, and frankly, I consider it rude for them to hold one under Tulsi's nose."

"You got it," Barbra said. "I see that orchid plant on your windowsill is dying. I'll take that with me and nurse it back to health."

Tulsi was stunned. The audacity of the staff to plan a shower in the building but not invite her! Barbra exited Hannah's office. Seeing Tulsi standing there, no doubt a shell-shocked look on her face, she held up the pot of brown leaves. "Tulsi! She's nearly killed another one, I think."

Barbra gave her a cheesy smile and headed back to her office. Tulsi thought better of discussing any issue with Hannah. Clearly, she was already aware of the situation and was trying to remedy it.

She bumped into Valerie on her way back to her office. "Hey, you got a few minutes?" Tulsi blurted out. She hadn't meant to discuss the situation with Valerie, but in her heart, she thought Valerie needed to know about the gossip. What she did with the information was her business.

Valerie's face flashed a pained expression. "Yes, Dr. Anthony. I have a few minutes."

They stepped into Tulsi's office and she closed the door before gesturing Valerie to take a seat on the couch.

"Is there something wrong?" Valerie asked as she sat, biting her lower lip.

Tulsi sat down on the other end of the couch. "I want to tell you something I overheard Dr. Mueller saying to Megan yesterday."

Valerie nodded. "Okay?" She looked uncomfortable sitting there. Her eyes were wary, her hands stiffly clenched in her lap.

"It seems Dr. Mueller is under the impression you are getting married so quickly because you're pregnant. That is what she told

Megan." Tulsi spoke as softly as she could. There wasn't an easier way of telling the poor woman.

Valerie's eyes widened, and her mouth dropped open. "What? I'm not pregnant. We just don't see any point in dragging the engagement out."

Tulsi pressed her palms together. "I understand that, and believe me, I do agree with you. Elaborate weddings just don't make much sense."

From the look on Valerie's face and the distant look in her eyes, her mind was churning. "Who else heard this fake gossip?" She stared back at Tulsi, a hard glint in her eyes.

"I did overhear Alissa and Clarissa discussing it. I don't know about any of the others."

She was silent a few moments before she said, "I... I'm not sure what I'm going to do with this information, but I thank you for telling me."

Tulsi gave her a gentle smile. "I'm sorry to be the bearer of such news, but I thought you needed to know."

CHAPTER TWENTY-SEVEN

"How's it going, Cortland?" Tulsi asked as the three women had their online meet-up. This time, on Friday, after work hours for Hannah and Tulsi.

"It's been a struggle. I finally got the electrical situation in the livestock barn fixed. Cost me an arm and a leg, but I shouldn't have to worry about another fire." Cortland grinned as though trying to make light of her situation. "How's married life treating you, Hannah?"

Hannah brushed away a loose strand of blonde hair. "It's like before the I-do's but without the guilt of living in sin. Maggie Mae and Toby, the dogs, don't notice any difference." Hannah hesitated momentarily, adding, "Cort, I have something to tell you."

Tulsi's grin grew ear to ear. It wasn't fair Cortland was left out of the loop. But Tulsi relished knowing the scoop earlier than Cortland and the rest of the clinic staff. "You're never going to guess!"

Cortland's nose wrinkled as she thought. "Well, you can't be preggers, so what else is there?"

Hannah laughed. "I *am* preggers!"

Cortland's mouth dropped open, her face reflecting her total surprise. "OMG! Hannah! What the—" She slapped her hand over her mouth.

Hannah shrugged. "I know, I was just as surprised. Totally flabbergasted. I'm due on Valentine's Day."

Tulsi scowled. "You didn't tell me that!"

Hannah laughed. "I know, I wanted something to surprise you with, too. So I didn't say anything. Besides, Andrew and I found out the tentative due date earlier this week."

"So what are you going to do? I mean, about the clinic and all?" Cortland asked. "Sorry, but I can't be running back and forth to cover the clinic for your maternity leave. Who will take care of my farm? And besides, it's a very long commute."

Hannah laughed and nodded. "I understand. I'm hoping Tulsi and Frances can hold down the clinic for me after labor and delivery day."

A snort escaped Tulsi's throat. "Ugh, Frances. That woman." She huffed her frustration. "Have you seen the newsletter article Frances wrote about herself?"

"Not yet." Hannah's tone was wary. "Do I dare ask?"

She tried to control it, but a smug smile spread across her face. "It's very thorough. Five pages long, all about herself, her education, and her theory on animal care. Quite enlightening."

Cortland started laughing so hard tears ran down her face. "Oh my God, I *can* believe it!"

Hannah rolled her eyes as she shook her head. "I told her less than one and a half pages." She groaned. "I'll talk to Barbra and ask her to whittle it down to one page. She will only be here for weekend, vacation, and holiday coverage."

Cortland piped in, "Have her remove any 'theories' that don't mesh with our clinic's mission statement. We don't need a maverick diluting it."

Tulsi cut in, "Did you know she's insinuating that Valerie and Craig are rushing to get married because she's pregnant?"

Scowling, Hannah's face turned red. "What? Are you kidding me?" Her brow furrowed as she looked at Tulsi through the laptop screen. "Did she really say that?"

Tulsi nodded. "I overheard Dr. Mueller telling Megan, and two of the staff were talking about the fake gossip a little later."

"I should hope not," Hannah cried. "Is it fracturing the staff?"

Tulsi gave a reluctant nod. "Between Frances and the staff? Yeah." The elation that surged through her at the situation made her almost giddy. "Valerie should rescind Frances's invitation to the wedding. Who would blame her?"

Needing to change the subject now that she'd let the boss know what was happening with the staff, she asked, "Cortland, have you heard about Dawson?"

Cortland controlled her face well enough but Tulsi could see the dimming in her eyes at the mention of his name. "He's going to Ohio. What more is there to say?" She squeezed her eyes together and swiped her face with her hands. "He made his choice, and it wasn't me."

It was Hannah's turn to change the subject. "On the other hand, Tulsi is infatuated with Lucas."

A fiery, hot blush flooded Tulsi's cheeks. "He's such a darling. It's not going to last, though."

Shock filled Hannah and Cortland's faces. "But you two got along so well! Especially at the wedding reception." Cortland gave Tulsi a wink and an ear-to-ear grin.

With a sigh, Tulsi explained, "His mother and all of his family don't like me. They want him to marry a Puerto Rican girl. His father, Graham, is nice, and he might be trying to smooth the rug behind the scenes." She shook her head, her nerves riddled with angst over the situation. "Did you know Lucas is half Puerto Rican and half Scottish?" Seeing her friends' shocked faces, she continued. "It doesn't make sense that Mrs. Campbell, who had her own happy marriage outside her culture, might want to prevent her son from having one." Tulsi's face scrunched. "If Mr. and Mrs. Campbell's marriage is so deep and strong, why would she adamantly discourage Lucas from marrying outside his culture?"

"Maybe she's not as content as she professes?" Cortland commented, obviously searching for a plausible reason for her behavior.

Tulsi frowned. "That's just it. From what little I saw, they're truly in love, with a strong friendship and partnership. I might agree if that weren't the case. They are a united front."

"Except when it comes to Lucas's future?" Hannah mused. "Maybe there's something special about Lucas? Is he the baby of the family?"

"Or maybe she's overprotective of him?" Cortland interjected.

Tulsi threaded her fingers through her hair as if pulling a chunk out. "He's the middle of five. Marco is the baby." She didn't want to let on that she knew the reason. Not yet. Lucas deserved a chance to explain about his former girlfriend himself. "She was downright mean and hurtful at the wedding reception."

The three of them were silent before Hannah said, "I'll ask around." Seeing the horror on Tulsi's face, she added, "Discreetly, of course. Someone must have an idea what's behind this protectiveness."

Tulsi waved. "Hey, I got to go. I'm meeting Lucas at the Irish Harp in thirty minutes. Let's talk again in a few weeks, okay?"

Tulsi scurried to put away her laptop and put a final polish on her lipstick when her doorbell rang.

Thinking Lucas had changed his mind and was picking her up, she hurried down the hallway and threw open the door.

It wasn't Lucas.

The handsome man standing before her was Indian. His plain black tie, crisp white button-down dress shirt, black dress pants, and wing-tip shoes made her think he was a Jehovah's Witness. His mouth parted slightly as he stared at her.

When he didn't say anything, Tulsi asked, "Who are you?" She didn't have time for this, whatever it was. She glanced at her watch and frowned. If she left this minute, she'd be on time.

Remembering whatever it was he had to say, the young man slipped his fingers in his pants pockets. "I'm your brother."

CHAPTER TWENTY-EIGHT

Tulsi blinked, her mind swirling with a jumble of thoughts that didn't make sense. He continued to stare at her, his eyes boring into hers, his stance uncomfortable as he shifted his weight slightly from foot to foot. "You're not my brother, Thomas."

He shook his head and pursed his lips. "No, I'm your biological brother. Kamal Vyan Patel." He pressed his hands together in prayer and bowed. "Namaste."

All thought fled her brain. Tulsi gripped the door jamb as her knees weakened and her pulse thundered.

Kamal reached for her arm as if to steady her but retracted his hand before touching her.

"Don't," she whispered, her eyes searching his face. He would not meet her eyes. Her suspicion grew. "What proof do you have?"

He held out an envelope he'd pulled from his shirt pocket. "Proof," he said.

Tulsi took it. Inside was a copy of a surrender document naming the same adoption agency that had handled her case. Tulsi Patel was the child's name; her age and birthdate were noted.

She had seen her adoptive parents' copy of the adoption paperwork. She knew Patel had been her original surname. Anjali Kumhar was listed as the person giving her up. She hadn't known that fact. Her knees wobbled again, and she grasped the door frame.

"May I come in now?" Kamal asked. Tulsi barely nodded before he stepped over the threshold, closing the door behind him. He turned to look at her again. "I am sorry to have frightened you. It was not my intent." He flashed a grin that disappeared fast when she didn't respond. "I was hoping my arrival would not overwhelm you. Nani, Anjali Kumhar, told me to contact you after she died."

"Nani? Was she my mother?" Tulsi's brain froze at the familiarity of the word in her mouth. Closing her eyes, she tried to follow flashes of memory spun as fine as a cobweb. A gray-haired woman bending over her, picking her up, spooning something orange and sweet into her mouth. Was it mango? Tulsi remembered tasting the intense sweetness of the fruit. Was that the real reason why she didn't like that tropical fruit?

"Nani was our maternal grandmother," he said. "I'm sorry to tell you she died two weeks ago."

She pressed her hand to her forehead and closed her eyes. The memories were dark. In the arms of someone she didn't know, screaming, crying, reaching out, and trying to escape while the woman who fed and played with her stood in the doorway before shutting the door. She never saw that woman again. The memories after that day were tangled, dark with flashes of faces like a nanosecond glimpse of a scene when illuminated by lightning. Tulsi pressed her arms over her abdomen.

"Are you okay?" Kamal asked.

"How did you find me? How did you know where I live?"

"It might be best if you sit down." He gestured to the couch. "May I sit down before I explain?" Tulsi nodded and teetered unsteadily toward a chair.

Facing her across the room, he started to explain. "Nani, my grandmother tracked you down using these surrender papers she signed when you were three. She tried to stay apprised of your life. The internet has made that easier in the last twenty years. When she fell sick, she told me to find you after she died."

Thousands of questions zipped through her mind like a kicked hornet's nest. Her hands on her knees, her eyes closed, she tried to steady her breathing. "I had no idea I was being followed."

Kamal shrugged. "Well, not followed exactly. But every so often, she would search the internet to see what popped up when she googled your name. The Anthonys never changed it. When something new showed, she told me." He smiled gently. "She was happy you became a veterinarian. She loved animals."

"Did my parents know? My adoptive parents, I mean."

When Kamal shook his head, Tulsi stood up and began to pace the small open space of the combined living, dining, and kitchen area. "Why? Why did she keep track of me?" After a few seconds, a motive for this madness crossed her mind. "Are you here for money? I don't have any. Maybe you should leave now." She walked to the door, shaking her head, breathing faster. Reaching the doorknob, she turned to Kamal.

Kamal's face was pale. He stood abruptly, stopping her. "Wait, no. That's not it."

Tulsi crossed her arms over her chest. "Well, what is it then?"

He gestured to the chair she had been sitting in while he resumed sitting on the couch. "I am here because you are the only known family I have left in America. Nani wanted me to seek you out, try to connect with you. And she asked me to see if you would be so kind as to do a favor for her."

Seriously? This woman, her grandmother, the one who relinquished her, wanted her assistance? "What's the favor?" Tulsi's eyes narrowed as she waited for the answer.

Kamal bowed his head as if in prayer. "Nani died two weeks ago of heart disease. A letter containing her final wishes was delivered by her attorney. She wants both of us to take her ashes home to the town of Kishunganj in India and scatter them there where she grew up." He quickly added, "Money was set aside for the plane fare and hotel. It won't cost you much. Only food, which is cheaper there." He stared at her, his voice imploring.

"Where is that?"

"It's in the east, near the Nepal and Bangladesh borders."

TULSI'S FLAME

Tulsi closed her eyes and buried her face in her hands. Tears started to drop into them. The rising knot in her gut became an ugly cry bursting from her tight chest and screwing up her face.

He waited patiently for her to regain her composure. "I am sorry. Nani wanted us to finally get to know each other. She hoped one day we might act like the siblings we are."

Looking up, without thinking Tulsi blurted out, "What about our mother? What about our father?" She paced frantically this time, her feet blindly carrying her from one end of the apartment to the other as questions and thoughts boiled inside her. "Assuming you are who you say you are, you would know where they are."

A pained expression flooded Kamal's face, scrunched features that drew in as if trying to mitigate pain. He pressed his lips together and hesitated, staring at her. Just when Tulsi thought he would refuse to divulge the information, he said, "I know exactly where they are... in cemeteries on different continents."

Tulsi reached for the chair and stumbled to sit down as flakes of stars swirled in her head. She tried to speak, but the aridness in her mouth and throat prevented it. When she looked into Kamal's eyes, he nodded sympathetically. "What...how...when?" she choked out.

"When you were two and I was only months old. It was called an accident, but I believe it was really murder or suicide."

Hot tears sprouted, running down Tulsi's cheeks. She covered her face and bent over, putting her head between her knees. He continued to speak as she sobbed.

"Our mother and father wanted to get married. Nani was all for it, but Ayra's family refused the marriage plan. Our mother, Mariamma, was of a lower caste. Ayra's family did not want their firstborn son to marry such a woman." He sat back against the cushions, recalling the details, pain emanating from his face. "They ran away to America with Nani and married here. You were born months later, and I was born nearly two years later." He cleared his throat and sighed, wiping moisture from under his eyes. "Our father's family tracked them down and tried to run our mother over as she crossed the street. Our parents fled in their car, perhaps being chased. Their car hit a bridge abutment."

Tulsi sat up, her voice contorted from her crying. "That sounds more like a homicide."

Kamal shrugged. "Perhaps, but I think they knew it was over. They were out of money and out of Nani's house to keep us safe. Nani was taking care of us while they were looking for someplace to live free from fear and retribution. I personally think they aimed for that bridge. Rational? Maybe not. The road was clear, and there weren't any witnesses. But the funny thing is, when the police inspected their car, it had bullet holes. Fresh ones, without rusty edges."

"Maybe they were shot at and lost control of the vehicle?"

"Could be." He paused as if assessing his next words. "Neither one of them had bullet wounds." He paused long enough to wipe his nose with a handkerchief pulled from his pocket. "After the accident, Ayra's family took his cremains back to India for burial. I don't know where. Our mother is buried in a Paterson, New Jersey cemetery."

They both were silent, absorbing the facts laid out in the open air of the small condo. Tulsi searched his features, looking for similarities with her own. His eyes and hair color were the same as her own. Then she noticed the birthmark at the tail end of his right eye. The small, four-millimeter dark brown circular nevus looked exactly like her own and in the exact same spot. As farfetched as the entire story sounded, it was such a distinct feature, he had to be telling the truth.

Tulsi had one more question. "Why was I given up for adoption, but you were not?"

He shrugged. "Nani told me once she couldn't keep us both."

"But why me and not you?" Tulsi reiterated, her voice stern and demanding. "Was it a gender decision?" Tulsi knew India had a history of infanticide of female fetuses and infants.

Kamal opened his mouth to answer just as Tulsi's cell phone rang.

CHAPTER TWENTY-NINE

"Where are you? Are you okay?" Lucas yelled through the phone, forcing Tulsi to pull the phone from her ear. She raised her index finger to Kamal before retreating to her bedroom for privacy. "I got delayed by an unexpected visitor."

Lucas sounded incredulous. "You couldn't call me? I've been sitting here at the bar nursing a beer for thirty minutes."

Tulsi cupped her forehead, a headache raging beneath. "I'm sorry. I've had some....extraordinary news."

"Oh," Lucas's tone softened. "I'm sorry. I should have known it was something important."

"I don't want to go out anymore. Can you come here?" Tears welled in her eyes again as she pleaded.

"Yes, of course. Whatever you need. I'll be there in ten," he said. "See you there. Love you."

"Love you, too," Tulsi said and disconnected. When she looked up, Kamal was standing in the bedroom doorway. He fidgeted and wrung his hands like he couldn't figure out where to put them.

"I should get out of your way. I guess I got you into trouble." He clasped his hands together. "I'm at the hotel near the highway. Can I give you my phone number?"

Tulsi nodded, unable to speak and not knowing what to say.

Kamal gave her the number, and she saved it in her contacts. Remembering her manners, she said, "I'll give you a call when I figure out—"

He held up his hand to stop her. "I understand. This has been a hard conversation for both of us. I'm planning to return to New Jersey in four days. My evening flight leaves on Tuesday at eight. Feel free to call me anytime." He mashed his lips together, "Perhaps we can meet for lunch or dinner to talk more before I leave?"

"Perhaps. I'll let you know." Tulsi walked him to the door. They both paused, unsure how to part. Should she give him a hug? A kiss on the cheek, or a handshake? He solved her dilemma by pressing his palms together. "Namaste," he said with a bow. He immediately turned and walked toward the parking lot.

As Tulsi watched, Kamal passed Lucas on the sidewalk. The men eyed one other as though sizing each other up. Neither one said anything.

Lucas walked through her still open door. "Who the heck was that?" Curiosity filled his face.

"He claims to be my biological brother," Tulsi whispered as if disbelieving the last hour had ever transpired. Was it all a dream? A nightmare?

"Whoa! Holy crap! Do you believe him? Is he legit?" Lucas asked, taking Tulsi in his arms.

She rested her head on his shoulder. "I don't know. He answered a lot of my questions." She huffed, "I have my last name, though. My original last name." She suddenly realized she could check the validity of his stories using her last name. And with Nani's full name, she could check probate records in New Jersey. Maybe even find her mother's grave. *How many cemeteries are there in Paterson, New Jersey?*

She clung to Lucas, letting his strength and love seep into her being, filling her with the support she needed. Hannah and Cortland were having their own issues. This...this revelation would have to be her own to explore and verify.

"What did he want? Money?" Lucas asked after kissing her forehead.

Tulsi pulled back and kissed him on the lips. "Surprisingly, no. He wants me to go to India with him to bury his grandmother. Our grandmother, if the story holds true."

"Is he serious? This unknown guy asks you to fly with him to India, and you're considering it?" His incredulous tone made her stop short.

"If he checks out, maybe. According to him, he and I are the only family on this side of the Atlantic. It might be nice to get to know him."

Lucas's voice turned stern. "And he might be a con artist. Lord knows what he'd do if he were alone with you."

Tulsi pressed her palm into Lucas's chest. "Don't worry, I'm not stupid. I'll vet him as best I can before deciding whether to go or not."

Satisfied, Lucas asked, "I have something important to tell you, too. I was going to spring it on you at the Harp, but—"

"Give me a minute to get us something to drink," Tulsi said. "I'm parched."

Tulsi returned to the couch where Lucas had settled, beer cans in hand. "Tell me."

"Remember I didn't get the lieutenant's position?" When she nodded, he continued. "Another has opened up."

"What! That's excellent, right? You don't have to re-test or anything, correct?"

Lucas smiled. "Nope." He held up his beer, and they clinked their cans together in celebration. "There's bad news too. They're placing someone from Station Three in Dawson's position. Which means this position would be there, at Station Three. Exactly where I didn't want to be."

"But you're going to be a lieutenant! That's amazing, Lucas. I'm so happy for you." She flung her arms around him and kissed him. Excitement over his promotion spilled out in her words. "You can handle Station Three. Perhaps they're looking for someone to help straighten the place out." She kissed his cheek. "I think they made a brilliant choice. When do you start?"

His news filled Tulsi's soul with relief. It had bothered her when he hadn't received the last promotion. Her worry stemmed from Dawson's leaving. When Dawson wasn't promoted to District Deputy Chief, he'd left the department entirely, seeking a job in Ohio. Cortland had been furious. She understood that anger. If Lucas had made the same decision to leave Colby Fire Department, Tulsi knew their relationship would be over. She could never leave Hannah and the clinic, not now. She was whole-heartedly invested in helping Hannah with the place. Despite the issues with the staff, their time working together meant the world to her even after this short period.

"Soon. I start August 11th."

"Does this mean a raise?"

Lucas raised an eyebrow. "It does. More money means..." He drum rolled on his leg with his index fingers, "I'm going to order my new truck! And I'll be getting my house sooner. Like as soon as possible."

"I like both of those ideas." She more than liked it. She loved the idea of not having to bump into his mother. She set her beer down beside his and took his hand. "I need you to tell me more."

"But you haven't told me about your visitor," Lucas reminded her.

"I have a question of my own to ask you," Tulsi said. "A question I've wanted to ask you for a while."

Lucas tensed, his shoulders slightly hunching before he nodded, "Ask away."

"Tell me about your relationship with Samantha." Tulsi grasped his hand as she said it. She didn't want him to think she was being judgmental.

His free hand rubbed the side of his face. "Samantha was a girlfriend. We started dating, and it was pretty hot and heavy. I was infatuated with her. She asked me to move in with her after a couple of months, which I did. Then, a week later she told me she got fired from her job. So, being a nice guy, I told her not to worry, I'd help with expenses more until she got another job."

He shrugged. "Except she never got another job. And before I knew it, I was paying for everything, on my cook's salary at the diner. Anyway, it became clear she wasn't looking for a job. When she asked for access to my credit card, I broke it off."

"Did you love her?" Tulsi asked, still holding tight to his hand.

TULSI'S FLAME

"I thought so then, but afterward, I saw it differently. She was like a shiny new toy. My first girlfriend and the opposite of what my mother was pushing toward me. Perhaps that was part of the attraction. In the end, she broke me, literally and figuratively. She also didn't want to have children. I want a big family, just like the one I grew up in. So, no, I don't regret breaking it off."

"Thanks for telling me," Tulsi whispered.

Lucas kissed her. "Your turn to tell me about this dude."

Still holding his hand, she stood up and led him down the hall to the bedroom. "I need you to hold me while I explain my story."

On her neatly made bed, they settled face to face. Lucas put his arms around her and tightened his grip. Tulsi rubbed her face against his shirt before settling down. They lay like that while Tulsi told Lucas about her visitor and what was said. She opened her heart and told him everything she remembered of those early years and of her fears, struggles, and hopes as she grew up knowing of her adoption.

Hours later, Tulsi drifted off in a troubled sleep while Lucas held her, chewing over everything she'd told him.

CHAPTER THIRTY

Tulsi was late for work on Saturday. Something that had never happened before. "You okay?" Hannah held up her cell phone as Tulsi came rushing in. "I was just about to call you."

Her arms filled with a purse, laptop, and a shopping bag, Tulsi struggled through the door and leaned against the wall, out of breath. "Help."

Hannah reached out and grabbed her oversized grocery bag. "Geez, what do you have in this thing?"

"A weeks' worth of snacks and beverages," Tulsi said over her shoulder as she led the way to her office and dropped everything on her desk.

Hannah set down the lunch tote, staring intently at her. "You didn't answer me...are you okay?"

"What makes you think something is wrong? What could possibly be wrong?" Tulsi said, trying to evade. She didn't want to talk about the situation yet. While she had fallen asleep easily, it hadn't eluded her later in the night despite Lucas's loving arms. His soft snoring was comforting, just knowing he was there, spooning against her back. Still, she relived her conversation with Kamal. Was he telling the truth? She figured she should be able to get Nani's probate and death records and her mother and father's death records. A double fatality accident should have been reported in the newspapers and at the police department. So many threads needed verifying, she started out of bed to begin the search on her laptop. But Lucas had stirred, reaching out to pull her back to bed, and she crawled back under the covers with him instead.

"I thought I'd go to Valerie's wedding, but now, not such a good idea," Hannah said, setting the bag down in the hallway.

Tulsi eyed her boss. Hannah's face was paler than Tulsi had ever seen it. "You don't look so well. You're a little green." Tulsi said just

TULSI'S FLAME

before Hannah bolted for Tulsi's office bathroom. *Ugh. Being pregnant must really suck.* She followed Hannah and held her hair back while her friend barfed up some pale stuff. "What did you eat?"

"Saltines. I heard they would stay down. I guess not." Hannah's voice was weak, trembling as she wiped her mouth on the towel Tulsi handed her. She sat back on her heels on the ceramic tiled floor. "Now. What about you?"

"I—I had something happen last night. I need to tell you and Cortland together because I don't want to have to repeat this story."

Hannah gave her a dubious look. "Is it something good or bad?"

"I'm not sure yet," Tulsi said, holding out her hand to help Hannah up. "Can we get Cortland on Zoom for an emergency meeting over our lunch break?"

"You can try. Send her a text message. She'll see it."

A normal load of back-to-back patient appointments kept Tulsi and Hannah busy all morning. Before ten o'clock, Valerie arrived and stopped Tulsi in the hallway.

"Can you spare me a minute?" Valerie asked, her bashful manner suggesting something was definitely up. Her white, billowy tea dress and white flip-flops confirmed Tulsi's suspicion the wedding was happening today. *Or was it?*

"Yes, of course." Tulsi gestured for them to step into a vacant exam room and shut the door. "What can I do for you?"

Valerie's eyes widened. "You've been good to me at the clinic. You took time to explain things and answer my questions. You've taught me a lot and always made me feel like part of the team. I've not treated you well, and I'm sorry about that. You deserve better." She clasped her hands together, an apologetic expression on her lovely face. I know it's late, but I want to thank you personally and give you this." She pulled an envelope out of her dress pocket and held it out.

A knot slid up Tulsi's throat. "Please tell me you're not giving your notice."

"No, it's not my resignation. It's a wedding invitation. I realize it's super short notice, and you're on duty today, but if you're free at noon...I'd really appreciate it if you could come."

When her breath returned, Tulsi nodded. "I'd love to come. I'll be there if I can, but don't count on it. I have patients scheduled all morning and Hannah isn't feeling well."

"Thank you. I'm sorry I didn't trust you initially. I should have. If you are a friend of Hannah and Cortland, you must be a good human. I'm sorry it took Frances's malicious gossip for me to see that. But I'm grateful to you for speaking with Hannah about it. Everyone on staff is." She leaned forward conspiratorially, "Frances won't be there. I rescinded her invitation." Valerie winked.

Blinking rapidly, Tulsi grasped Valerie's hand. "I'm sorry it happened, but I'm glad I could help." Tulsi spread her arms open. "Hug for good luck?"

Valerie nodded, and they hugged briefly. "If I don't get there, you have a beautiful wedding," Tulsi said before letting her go.

The three friends connected during lunch. Tulsi, who arranged the trio's emergency meeting, spoke first. "Ladies, you are never going to guess what happened last night."

Cortland took the bait. "Lucas proposed?"

"Nope. A guy showed up at my door claiming to be my biological brother." She watched as her words settled in. By the horrified expressions on their faces, the open-mouthed, wide-eyed stares, she knew her words had hit.

"Holy cow! Tulsi, what did you do?" Hannah asked.

Tulsi told them the entire story of Kamal's visit and everything he'd told her. "He gave me his full name and his phone number. I did some identity verification. So far, it's all been legit."

"Are you going to go to India with him to return Nani's ashes?" Cortland asked.

TULSI'S FLAME

Tulsi chewed on her lower lip. "I haven't decided. I haven't had time to check about Nani. Until I can confirm everything, I'm holding off making that decision."

Hannah said, "It would seem creepy to travel so far away with someone you hardly know."

"True. I'm inclined to say no. But I'd rather have my reasons defined first."

Cortland asked, "Was this Nani the one who gave you up for adoption?"

"According to the surrender paperwork, yes. I had just asked Kamal why when Lucas called. I never got a satisfactory answer from him."

Hannah sat quietly, listening to Cortland and Tulsi over the Zoom connection. "If this Nani was the one who gave you up, will you go on this mission?"

Tulsi shrugged, "I don't know. I guess it will depend on her reasons for giving me up while keeping Kamal."

"Maybe because he was the male... primogenitor and all that," Cortland said. A chorus of donkeys brayed in the background. Behind her was a big window looking out into the paddock area. Cortland glanced out the window.

"You have donkeys?" Hannah asked. "I love them! I'm so jealous."

Tulsi directed a response to Cortland. "That was my first thought, too. Maybe Nani thought she could finagle some money or prestige of some variety for Kamal. Make his father's family pay out."

"Doesn't sound like they had any interest in Ayra's offspring," Hannah interjected.

Tulsi slowly nodded. "True."

Cortland glanced over her shoulder again. "Looks like I better get outside before the donkeys tear down the gate. Tulsi, let me know what you decide."

"I will. As soon as my questions are answered."

Frances left Hannah's office in tears after appointment hours closed. She gave Tulsi an embarrassed glance before ducking her head and retreating to her own office on the second floor. Knowing what must have happened, Tulsi knocked lightly on Hannah's door before entering.

"Hey, you okay?" Tulsi knew Hannah had too much heart to want to discipline anyone. She usually let Barbra Pari handle behavioral issues. But this had been something she, as owner of the clinic, wanted to do herself.

Hannah scrubbed her face before speaking. "Yeah. I gave her an ultimatum. Find another job before September or I'll fire her. I can't have her derisive gossip mucking up our staff."

Tulsi sat across from Hannah's desk. "Wow, I hadn't expected you to fire her or force her to leave. But you make a good point. We're a small band. We need to trust and respect each other to care for our patients and their owners." She eyed her boss and friend. "So what now?"

"You mean about covering me during maternity leave?" Hannah asked.

Nodding, Tulsi said, "I'll never be able to handle this place on my own."

"That's why I gave her until September first to leave, one way or the other. I'll start advertising and interviewing for the position immediately. Hopefully, it will be a seamless transition. That will give the new vet five and a half months to get accustomed here." She paused before whispering, "What are you going to do? When would that trip to India be if you decided to go?"

Tulsi rubbed her palm over her face while shaking her head. "I expect it would be soon."

"Well, let me know as soon as you can." Hannah slapped her hand to her forehead. "I almost forgot about the Colby Festival. It's Saturday,

August 17th this year. Frances was going to cover the booth, but not anymore. Can you cover it?"

Tulsi wrinkled her nose. "How about I cover the clinic and *you* cover the booth? Or maybe two staff members can handle it? You know how I am with the public. I'm an introvert. I don't like crowds and strangers."

"I promised the town manager we'd staff the booth with a vet. I don't want to be at the booth. Especially with this morning sickness making my every waking moment miserable." She paused briefly before adding, "Besides, you need to get out more. I know you want to be a seamless part of this community. Trust me, it will be a good step toward that."

Hannah hit the sweet spot. She knew Tulsi wanted to be accepted by the community. To be seen as an individual, a human being with much the same wants and needs as her white American counterparts. Tulsi grumbled, "All right. I'll do it." A thought popped into her head. "Hey, you know, maybe we could try telemedicine appointments. Especially for those appointments that can be done on a video consultation basis. That vet office in Louisiana I was working in was trying it just before I left them. They were pretty happy with it."

Hannah's face brightened. "Hmm, that's interesting. I could do it from home while on maternity leave." She scribbled something down on a notepad. "I'll have Barbra look into it."

Tulsi lay her head back against the cushion and closed her eyes. With a heavy sigh, she said, "Lucas said something to me a week or so ago that has me..." she shrugged before adding, "concerned. I guess that's the best word for it."

Hannah rose and sat down beside her. "What was it?"

"Lucas told me to forget about his family's cold shoulder. He loves me." When Hannah's eyes opened wide and she smiled, Tulsi held up her palm. "No, wait. Don't congratulate me yet. He hasn't asked." She stopped for a minute, trying to remember his words. "He said, 'Only you matter to me. I'll be happy as long as you're with me.'"

"Isn't that great news?"

Tulsi shook her head. "I never told you about running into his mother in the restroom at the quinceañera."

Again, Hannah's eyebrows rose high, her eyes widening. She reached out and held Tulsi's hand.

"She told me to stay away from her son." A shiver ran down Tulsi's spine as she recounted the memory.

"Oh my, do you think she means it? What would she do? Hurt you?"

Tulsi stood and began pacing the small office. "I doubt she'd hurt me, but I don't know her well enough." She looked out the window. "She never threw Lucas out of the house when he kept seeing me. Maybe she's bluffing about that, too." The need to unburden her soul spurred her on. "Also, I heard why they are so protective of Lucas. Two of his relatives were talking in the restroom before his mother showed up." Tulsi turned toward Hannah. "He had a girlfriend a few years back. She invited him to move in with her, which he did, and then she lost her job. She had Lucas paying for everything: her apartment, utilities, food, her hair appointments, and manicures,—everything."

"Holy cow bells! What happened?" Hannah sat up straight.

"She asked him for his credit card in her name. He refused, so she broke up with him and threw him out."

"What audacity! Thank God he was smart enough to refuse. No wonder his family keeps close tabs on him." She rose and hugged Tulsi. "You're not like that."

"They don't know that. I guess they assume I'm after his money, too." She could see the gears in Hannah's brain whirring, trying to figure something out.

Her boss walked to the door slowly, ponderingly. Pausing with her back toward Tulsi, she abruptly spun around. "Why not invite them here? Do they have any pets that need checkups? You could be the one to care for them during the appointment." They would have to respect you after seeing how diligent you are as a veterinarian."

Tulsi wrinkled her nose. "I don't know. They could walk in, see me, and leave. And under what pretense would they bring their dog or cats in? Besides, I don't think they have any pets right now."

Hannah sighed. "I guess you're right. I'll think about it some more." She glanced at the clock on the wall. "Gosh, it's nearly seven p.m. I've got to get going before Andrew calls." Immediately, her cell phone rang. After glancing at it, she said, "speak of the devil himself."

As Hannah answered the phone, Tulsi returned to her office to retrieve her things and get home.

Little did she know what awaited her there.

CHAPTER THIRTY-ONE

Pulling into the condominium parking lot, Tulsi's ire rose at seeing another car parked in her parking spot. Only when she got closer did she recognize it. Her mother's BMW filled her space. From the look of it, her parents were inside the car waiting for her.

She steered her SUV to the nearest visitor space and got out to greet them as they approached her.

"There you are, dearling. I was afraid you would be out all night." Her mother threw her arms around Tulsi and hugged her gently before her father gave her a hearty squeeze.

"Just tied up at the office on some scheduling things," Tulsi replied, removing items from her car, which her father hefted to carry.

"Do tell us all about what's going on." Mrs. Anthony brimmed with excitement. "We especially want to hear all about your young man."

They followed her to the condo door, and she let them in. Her father set the cases down on her dining table as Tulsi continued to the fridge. "Want anything to drink?" She pulled a can of flavored seltzer out and held it in her mother's direction. Mrs. Anthony took it, and Tulsi handed her father a can of beer. Retrieving a can for herself, she led them into the living room area. "Have a seat. I'll be right back."

Tulsi escaped to her bedroom, quickly tearing off her scrubs, settling on a tee shirt and pulling on shorts. Slippers on her feet, she returned to the living space. "What brings you so far?" She settled herself in the chair beside the fireplace.

"We decided it was time to see your new place and meet your new beau," her mother bubbled, her enthusiasm tiring Tulsi out more. *How long are they going to stay and where?* Her condo was a one-bedroom. And she was on duty for the next week, including the weekend.

"Well, here it is. Where are you two staying?" It was always best to be forthright with her parents. Despite her mother being a psychiatrist, she wasn't good at reading between the lines. If Tulsi wasn't direct, her mother might try to wiggle her way into staying at her condo somehow.

Her father quickly replied, "We have a reservation at the local hotel."

Her mother added, "Yes, but we'll want to spend as much time with you as possible."

Tulsi squinted. She was going to have to break the news to them immediately. "I'm on duty for the next seven days. I can't be showing you around town or anything." She immediately regretted telling them more than necessary. Her mother would come up with some scheme, and in a minute flat, she didn't disappoint her daughter.

"Don't worry about us. We'll do some sightseeing around the area during the day. We'll catch up with you for dinner. Do you think your beau will be able to join us?"

"Sometimes I sleep in my office at the clinic when I'm on duty to monitor my surgical patients more closely. Besides, Lucas's schedule is erratic right now."

"Lucas, is it?" Her mother turned to her father. "Did you hear that, Nathan? His name is Lucas."

Her father mashed his lips together and nodded. It dawned on Tulsi he didn't look too pleased about being here. Perhaps her mother decided to come, and he came along to help Tulsi manage the intrusion.

"Can he meet us for dinner tonight?"

"Mom, I doubt it. Most likely, he's working. He just got a promotion, so he must work overtime."

"Oh, yes. He's a firefighter, isn't he?" her mother asked breathlessly.

"Yes." Tulsi steeled her nerves for the onslaught. Her mother responded as Tulsi anticipated. Mrs. Anthony started asking all manner of questions about Lucas, not giving Tulsi time to answer any of them.

The doorbell rang in the middle of her mother's chatter about Lucas's job. Mom clasped her hands together, glee radiating from her face. "Oh, maybe that's him now!" She stood and followed Tulsi to the door.

"Gwendolyn, come back here. Let Tulsi answer the door in private. Besides, she told you he was working." Her father followed after his wife, reaching out to grasp her arm and hold her back.

Tulsi prayed it wasn't Lucas, but she didn't know who it could be other than him. She opened the door.

Kamal.

"I'm so sorry to disturb you. I'm on my way to the airport. I decided to cut my stay here short. Basically, I wanted to know if you had made a decision yet."

Tulsi opened her mouth to reply, hoping to get Kamal away before the scene erupted.

Too late.

"Tulsi, is this Lucas?" Her mother's voice quivered as she stood a short distance from the doorway and stared at Kamal.

Tulsi turned to her mother, "No, this is Kamal." Realizing her flub up, she tried again, "It's not Lucas."

"Kamal?" her mother's eyes took him in head to toe and back with a worried look on her face.

Kamal stared at Tulsi as he said, "Yes, I'm Kamal, Tulsi's brother."

Mrs. Anthony fainted, right there on the carpeted floor. Tulsi's father tried to rouse his wife while Kamal and Tulsi looked on in horror.

"Perhaps I should leave," Kamal said softly.

She nodded vigorously. "It would be best. I'll call you later about the trip."

When her mother was alert and conscious again, Tulsi gave her a shot of tequila. It was all she had besides beer. It did the trick. Her mother regained her legs and waddled to the couch with her father's help. Sinking deep on the cushion, she muttered, "That man was your brother? Your biological brother?"

TULSI'S FLAME

Tulsi cringed at the strain in her voice and on her face. "Yes. He showed up here a couple nights ago and introduced himself."

Eyebrows pinched into one long brow, her father interjected, "Are you sure—"

Tulsi held up her hand. "Yes. I've checked out his identification. I believe he is who he says he is. My biological brother."

"But why? Why did he come looking for you now?" Mrs. Anthony asked, an edge in her voice.

Tulsi decided it would be easier to tell them the entire story.

Twenty minutes later, she finished. "That's what he wanted to know. If I would accompany him to India with Nani's ashes to spread them in her ancestral village."

"You aren't going, correct?" her father asked, trying to steer Tulsi's answer. He'd been silent during her story, probably thinking and mulling over the circumstances.

"I haven't decided yet, though I'm strongly disinclined to go." She shook her head. "She was the person who gave me up. Why should I elevate her to some sacred grandmotherhood after she did that to me? I never knew her, and she never knew me."

Her mother butted into the conversation. "I'm relieved he's not a boyfriend." She approached and took Tulsi's hand. "We've always wanted what's best for you. Having someone of the same…" she paused uncomfortably before adding, "to be blunt, of the same skin color, would lead to more harassment, alienation, and racism."

Tulsi thought her head would explode. Unable to hold her tongue, she blurted, "Like you're portraying now?"

Both parents reeled backward, their faces pale. Her mother looked as though she were going to cry. "Tulsi, we want you to have an easy life. It's not racism. It's wanting our daughter to not have any more problems."

Mr. Anthony put his hand on his wife's shoulder and interjected, "It's a moot point if Kamal isn't your boyfriend."

Her blood boiling and her spine stiffening, Tulsi said, "Oh, thank God my boyfriend isn't Indian. Lucas is Puerto Rican." Sarcasm dripped from her words. She was long past needing or wanting their approval. As much as she loved them and owed them for taking her in, she loathed their attitude. They thought of her as less than whole, less than acceptable. Only if she married a white American could they be pleased for her.

"Puerto Rican?" her mother gasped. She turned toward her husband. "That's not even American, is it?"

A hard knock on the door sounded as her father opened his mouth to reply.

They all froze, looking at it, but no one moved to answer it. What if it was Kamal again? The knock turned to pounding, longer and harder this time. Through the closed door, Tulsi heard Lucas calling, "Tulsi, I know you're in there. I saw your car. Open up!"

Mrs. Anthony's eyebrows and lids shot up before she edged closer to her husband. "Is it Kamal again?"

Tulsi's father's face tensed, his jaw hardening along with his stare. "Do you want me to get rid of him?" he said, rising to his feet.

Tulsi jumped up. "No. It's not Kamal. It's Lucas." She hurried to the door, hoping Lucas didn't knock again. It was out of character for him to yell through the door like that. Now was not the time to make a scene. She'd already had to deal with far too many unexpected visitors today.

She cracked open the door. There stood Lucas, decked out in his fire gear, his face tense and furious. "What the—"

"Get out. Now. There's a fire in the adjoining building." He grasped her arm, tightening his grip as he tried to haul her out the door.

"Wait! My parents, my purse!" Tulsi pulled her arm back.

Lucas pushed open the door so hard it bounced off the wall behind it with a crack and shouted, "Let's go. There's a fire."

CHAPTER THIRTY-TWO

Terror flooded through Lucas when the call came in. It was Tulsi's condominium complex, though the building name differed from hers. He didn't know where it stood in the nine-building complex, but he was afraid it was close to her building. He swore under his breath as the fire engine sped through town, not fast enough for his liking. The entire contingent of Station Two and Station One apparatuses were converging on the scene along with mutual aid fire departments. All the pre-planning they had done for just such an incident was suddenly put into real use. Every year, the department took them to large structures where pre-plans were set. It was their duty to remember exactly where each hydrant, alternate water source, and firebreak was located. Lucas was glad about that. After he'd found out Tulsi lived there, he'd studied the plans with added fervor. The nine buildings were arranged to shape a large letter three. Most of the building names, he couldn't remember.

"Let's go," he yelled again as the two people on the couch sat stunned.

Tulsi grabbed her purse and her laptop. With a shout of horror, she yelled, "Leo!" She turned to get her gecko, but Lucas grabbed her arm. "I'll get Leo. You get your parents out."

He headed down the hall, returning with Leo's tank as Tulsi and her parents exited the condo. "Go to your car and stay there." He unceremoniously handed Leo's cage to her father before briskly walking off to the next apartment.

CHAPTER THIRTY-THREE

Fear gripped Tulsi as she watched him go until the blare of more sirens behind her grabbed her attention. People milled about the parking area. Some trying to move their vehicles, clogging up the travel lanes, making it impossible for any of them to leave. Firefighters struggled to attach hoses to hydrants amid the chaos.

More fire trucks were entering the complex. An identical building belching smoke from a top floor window was to the right of Tulsi's building. She could see firefighters helping occupants evacuate, much like Lucas was doing. Some were breaking down doors to assure no one was left inside the structure.

Orange tongues of flames slipped out, searching for more oxygen. Multiple fire hoses shot into the broken windows. Tulsi could see firefighters breaking open the roof with axes, while a ladder truck reached overhead, ready to shoot water down onto the fire and the building's roof above the fire area. In another twenty minutes, more fire equipment was spewing thousands of gallons of water over the inferno. The flames refused to retreat, the smoke still billowing from the building's side, windows and the opened roof.

Tulsi and her parents watched silently as the battle continued for another hour. Once, she thought she saw Lucas. It had to be him. CAMPBELL-LOPEZ was written across the back of a firefighter's coat in reflective lettering. The hyphenated name surprised her. Wasn't Lucas's last name Campbell? She made a mental note to ask him about it later.

The police wrangled the crowd, clustering them beside the building farthest from the fire. They sat on the grass or walked glassy-eyed and stunned in the prescribed safe area. Dusk and finally night fell, as they all tittered about, trying to account for everyone they knew who should be there.

Tulsi sat with her parents.

Her father asked, "Was that fireman your Lucas?"

She nodded in response. Her parents looked at each other but said nothing.

They didn't speak for a long time, all stunned out of words as the conflagration swelled. Eight fire hoses spewed water for more than two hours before it eased and finally sputtered to a smoldering mess.

The entire time, Tulsi prayed Lucas was okay. That he wasn't hurt or trapped or running out of air like Dawson had experienced months before. The gut-wrenching terror of the entire evening kept her quiet, praying and, in the final stages, wondering if she could afford to care for Lucas so much and watch him do this every shift. Did she have the emotional capacity to let him go and then worry about him during every shift? Worrying constantly he might not come home to her? Ever?

"Tulsi." She wasn't sure if she was dreaming. At the sight of him, she was on her feet, running toward him. His fire coat hung open, smeared, and covered in soot. The chin strap dangling, his yellow fire helmet still sat on his head. His sweaty face was blackened with soot, except for a strip of white skin showing where the strap had been. The strong odor of smoke on his gear reached her before he did. She didn't care. She flung her arms around his neck and kissed him hard. He kissed her back, his arms clutching her like he'd never let her go.

"You're okay?" he demanded, looking her up and down. The tension in his face eased as he looked her over.

"I'm fine. Are you okay?"

"Tired, but better now that I know you're truly safe."

"Lucas?" her father asked, approaching them, her mom two steps behind.

Lucas turned. "Yes, I'm Lucas Campbell-Lopez, sir. I assume you're Tulsi's father."

"Indeed, Nathan Anthony." After her mom poked his side, he added, "This is my wife, Gwendolyn. Tulsi's mother."

Lucas swept his helmet off, inadvertently displaying sweat-saturated hair plastered to his head. Even the jaunty lock of hair that usually flopped in his eyes was pressed flat. "Pleased to meet you both. I'm very glad to know you're safe." He looked around. "Where's Leopold?"

Tulsi answered, "We left Leo in his aquarium tank inside my car. It should be warm enough in there for a few hours."

"Good place for him. At least he didn't have to inhale all that smoke."

"What happened? How did it start?" Mrs. Anthony asked timidly.

"That's up to the fire marshal to investigate and decide. If I had to guess, I'd say it was a candle or food on the stove that was forgotten or neglected. Fortunately, the occupants were able to escape and call us."

"When can we go back to my condo?" Tulsi asked, the emotional frenzy and the late hour combining to make her more tired than she'd been in years.

"Probably within the hour. We'll be here all night and into tomorrow, hosing down hot spots and smoldering debris. The fire was contained to the two top floor units, and another two beneath them. There's bound to be a lot of water damage to the rest of the building, but overall, it was a good save." He turned, hearing a firefighter whistle behind him. "I have to go. Nice to meet you, Mr. and Mrs. Anthony. Tulsi, I'll talk with you soon." He pressed a quick kiss against her lips before jogging away, his helmet in hand, his name emblazoned in reflective print on his coat, and Tulsi's heart.

"He's very brave," her father said, hugging his wife to him.

Tulsi studied their contrite-looking faces. "He's a good man. The bravest man I know. I love him, and he loves me."

Her father nodded. "We want to meet him under better circumstances." He looked down at his wife's face. "We should learn to trust your judgment." Her parents opened their arms to her, and she walked into them, grateful for their acquiescence.

CHAPTER THIRTY-FOUR

She was relieved to see no fire or water damage when she returned to her condo. However, the unit smelled strongly of smoke that had come in through an open window. Though the damage was already done, she closed it since smoke still emitted from untamed hot spots in the wreckage of the building next door. Before leaving, she grabbed the sealed container of Leo's food and yesterday's dirty scrubs.

"Come back to the hotel with us. We'll put you up in a room if there's one available," her father said. He pulled out his phone and called. Five minutes later, he hung up. "They're saving you a room."

Tulsi gathered some things for her overnight stay and drove to the hotel on Willard Street with her parents following.

On the way, she called Hannah despite the early morning hour. "I might not be in to work tomorrow. There's been a fire at my condo complex." She prayed her friend and boss didn't ask too many questions. Her body ached from all the tension, and her head didn't feel all that clear.

"Oh no!" Hannah shouted. "Are you okay?"

She nodded her head, though Hannah couldn't see her. "It didn't damage my unit, but the smoky smell is bad. I'll have to see about getting my condo and everything in it cleaned." She told Hannah she was staying the night at the hotel with her parents.

"Your parents are here too?"

"Yeah, they were there when it happened. It's been a crazy night. I'll explain more when I see you."

"Keep me informed. By the way, Frances isn't coming in anymore. Don't worry. I'll see what Barbra and I can do about the schedule."

"Thanks, Hannah. I'll be bringing my gecko to work too. I don't want him in that condo under those environmental conditions."

Next, she texted Lucas: 'I'm staying at the hotel tonight. Too much smoky smell at the condo. Stay safe. Love you.' She wasn't surprised he was too busy to answer her message.

Her parents and she split up at the hotel. Tulsi settled Leo's tank on the desk in her room and gave him fresh water and food. He looked up at her from the bottom of his tank appreciatively. Satisfied he was safe, she pulled off her stinky clothes and showered. Her hair still wet, she crawled under the covers and slept soundly.

Her phone alarm sounded at six a.m. After showering again to wash the lingering smoky scent out of her hair, Lucas called.

"Are you okay? Did you sleep okay?" His voice sounded drained and tired, but concerned. "I'm on my way over to your hotel."

"Good. You can carry Leo for me. I'll have to set him up in my office for the time being. Until my condo smells better." She dressed in the one set of scrubs she'd brought with her. They also reeked of smoke, but she could wash yesterday's scrubs in the clinic's laundry and change once they were dry.

Lucas enveloped her in his arms and crushed her to him when she opened the door. "I'm so glad you're okay."

Tulsi clung to him, not sure if the smoky odor was coming from his or her clothes. "Me too, I can't believe it all happened. I feel numb."

He stepped back to look at her. "You're in your scrubs. Going to work today?" his voice rose an octave with incredulity.

"No choice. Dr. Mueller left. If I don't go in, there's no one to see my patients. Besides, I have to check out of here this morning anyway."

• • • •

He eyed the room, seeing a paper bag already stuffed for transport. Leo scratched at his tank glass, looking for some attention. Lucas walked over and brought his face down to Leo's level. "Hey, buddy. I'm glad to see you're okay, too." He turned to Tulsi. "What about this guy?"

"He appears to be fine. I'll be able to keep an eye on him at work." She picked up her bag. "Can you carry him?"

Lucas jumped to assist, lifting the tank and following Tulsi to her SUV. "Where are you staying tonight?" he asked, putting Leo's cage on the floor in the front seat. He wished he had his own place so he could invite her to stay with him. Maybe it was time to move full speed ahead on finding a house. Seeing Tulsi returning to that condo complex would do nothing for his nerves. They'd been lucky this time. He didn't want her still living there in case there was another incident.

Tulsi shrugged. "Not sure. I'll let you know when I have time to figure it all out."

"What about your parents? Are they staying in town?"

"Considering the circumstances, they're returning home today. They said they'll be back in a few weeks. They want to meet my brawny and brave fireman."

Lucas chuckled. "You seeing someone else in the fire department?"

Tulsi swatted his butt. "Of course not."

He nodded and gave her another bear hug before she got behind the wheel and shut the door. He thought hard. Where could Tulsi say? A vision of his sisters' old room at his parents' house formed. The room was not used for anything important with both of them married and in homes of their own. "I have something in mind. I'll let you know."

CHAPTER THIRTY-FIVE

"But Mama, she needs a place to stay until her condo can be professionally cleaned. Why can't Tulsi use Maria and Arely's old room for a few days?"

His mother glared at him. "That's my quilting room now. We don't have room for her." She turned away and began gathering things for the breakfast meal.

His mother was exaggerating. She didn't want Tulsi anywhere near him or the house. He could ask if she could sleep on the roof, and the answer would be the same.

Before he could plead Tulsi's case further, his father walked into the kitchen.

As if registering the tension in the room, his father sat at the table and asked. "What's going on?"

His mother busied herself getting his coffee and breakfast ready.

Lucas told his father the story, the same one he'd told his mother not five minutes before. "She needs a place to stay until her condo can be cleaned of the smoky smell." Knowing how his father felt about Tulsi, he added, "I asked Mama if she could stay in Maria and Arely's old room, but..." He didn't need to repeat his mother's answer.

His mother set the cup of black coffee and the plate of bacon, eggs, baked beans, and broiled tomato on the table with a thud before her husband. He stared at it a minute before looking up at her as she walked away stiffly.

"Carmen, come here, please," he said quietly.

His mother set her dishtowel down on the counter and went to her husband's side. Her face hardened. He took her hand in both of his and squeezed it gently.

"We must help this young woman. It's the least we can do," he said, his brogue thick with emotion. "Remember how you took care of me when I needed a place to stay?"

Lucas's mother stared at her husband, her face softening and her shoulders slumping. "You were in a different situation when my parents took you in."

Mr. Campbell nodded. "That's true. But your father was kind enough to understand I couldn't find a place to stay in your village. The lone hotel was destroyed in the hurricane."

They stared at each other. Carmen wiped away a tear as it slid down her cheek before she nodded curtly. Lucas could sense the silence between them was ladened with conversation.

His father nodded to his wife. "Bring Tulsi over, and we'll set her up in the craft room. She can stay as long as she needs a place." Lucas's father said, "Let's all have dinner together tonight. Can you arrange it, Lucas?"

His mother opened her mouth, hardness in her face again as if she were going to object. But his father squeezed her hand. Meeting his wife's eyes, he said, "We need to get to know her better."

· · · ·

Lucas arrived at Tulsi's office in the early afternoon and could have knocked her over with a toothpick when he told her the plan. "You want me to stay under your mother's roof? Seriously?" The audacity of the suggestion made Tulsi laugh. Was Mama Campbell hoping to smother her in her sleep? Then she remembered Lucas didn't know about her mother's threatening words in the restroom at the quinceañera.

"It's my father's house too, and he rules the roost, despite what my mother says. It shouldn't take long to have your condo cleaned." Lucas asked from his seat on the couch. "Did you arrange for a cleaning crew?"

Tulsi nodded as she rocked in her desk chair. "I called them as soon as I got to work. They're coming on Tuesday." Her jaw tightened, thinking of staying at Lucas's family home for two days. "I think I'd be more comfortable sleeping here on the couch. Besides, Leo will be lonely if I don't stay with him."

Lucas jumped up and pulled her to her feet. "My parents want to get to know you. Don't say no." His voice cracked as he said, "Please give them a chance. I know they're going to love you as much as I do." He wrapped his arms around her and held her so close she could hear the staccato beating of his heart.

Dropping her head to his shoulder, she breathed in deeply. He smelled so fresh and clean, except for the tiniest, faintest odor of smoke still lingering in his hair. "You still smell a little smoky."

"I didn't use the SootSoap at the firehouse."

"SootSoap? Made for firefighters?"

He pulled back. "Yup. It works great." He plucked a stray clump of her hair and inhaled. "You could use some." He kissed her forehead, her nose, and finally her lips. "Now, stop diverting the conversation. You'll come stay in my sisters' room, right?"

Tulsi closed her eyes. A million bad scenarios about staying under the same roof with his mother flickered through her mind. But maybe, just maybe, his mother would see that Tulsi wasn't like his old manipulative girlfriend. She was a professional woman earning her own keep. She didn't need a man to fund her life. In fact, she didn't want one in that capacity. A handsome, sexy, quiet guy who took the time to understand and relish her introverted nature and was not put off by her silence. *A guy like Lucas.* "Okay. I'll stay there. Can I bring Leo?" Her eyes searched Lucas's features.

"Sure. He'll be a good boy, won't you Leo?" He stared at the leopard-spotted gecko. "I'm sure Mama's used to lizards, geckos, and iguanas from growing up in Puerto Rico." The glee in his voice was unmistakable. "I'll be back to help carry your stuff and this fella. We're expected for dinner tonight."

CHAPTER THIRTY-SIX

The room Tulsi settled into that evening was cute, with pale green walls and a floral border in tropical colors. A sewing machine beside the bed sat buried under a pile of fabric that might be an unfinished quilt.

Lucas set the aquarium tank on the dresser top. "You'll be more comfortable here than a hotel. My sisters used to have bunk beds, but Mama gave them to Arely when her twin boys outgrew their cribs. Mama uses this as a craft room, but she put her quilting away for you."

Grreat, I've put Mama Campbell out. "That was nice of her. I'm interested in quilting but never tried." Tulsi set her overnight bag on the bed.

"I'm sure she wouldn't mind teaching you." He pulled her into his arms and hugged her tight but let her go as the stairs creaked. "Someone's coming." He crossed the room to look out the window.

Mr. Campbell knocked on the open door frame. "Dinner will be ready in five minutes."

"Thanks," Lucas said, echoing Tulsi's thank you. "We'll be right down."

Mr. and Mrs. Campbell sat at either end of the dining room table. His mother had set the table with her finest china, silverware, and crystal. Marco, whom Tulsi had met when she first arrived, sat on one side of the table. Lucas and Tulsi sat side by side opposite him.

"Thank you very much for allowing me to stay here for a day or two. I appreciate your hospitality." Tulsi said rather stiffly. Small talk wasn't her forte, but she wanted to make sure they knew she was grateful for the invitation and wouldn't overstay her welcome.

Platters and bowls of food were passed clockwise around the table, allowing each person to take as much as they wanted. It was unlike growing up in her adoptive parents' home, where the maid brought in each plate already filled with the evening's dinner, like a restaurant. Tulsi's shoulders released some tension with the more casual meal style.

As if sensing she wouldn't know what some things were, Lucas told her what he was handing to her. A platter of pernil, bowls of guineitos con mollejas en escabeche, rice with beans, yams, and a garden salad. Tulsi took a polite couple of tablespoons of each dish, except for pernil, which smelled like roasted pork. She took a larger portion of it. "Mrs. Campbell, everything looks and smells amazing," Tulsi said, glancing down at her plate.

She whispered to Lucas, "What's this again?"

"It's a special dish often served during the Christmas holidays. Guineitos con mollejas en escabeche. Chicken gizzards with green banana in a vinegar, lemon juice, and oil-based sauce," Lucas whispered back.

Tulsi hardened the grin on her face. *Chicken gizzards? If this is some kind of prank Mrs. Campbell is playing on me, I can play along. Assuming I can choke it down.* "It looks delicious. Thank you."

Mrs. Campbell gave her a hard stare before saying, "Gracias."

A tense silence settled around the table. Tulsi had tried to be polite and kind. Why was the tension worse after complimenting Lucas's mother?

Mr. Campbell entwined his fingers and bowed his head. "Let us say grace."

Everyone else at the table did the same, so she did too.

"Gracious Father, we thank you for this wonderful food and the love of family. Amen."

They all said, "Amen."

Tulsi took a bite of the pernil. It was spicy, juicy, and delicious.

Mrs. Campbell pounced. "I wasn't sure you would eat the pork, considering your religion. Aren't you Muslim or Hindu or something?" Her eyes partially concealed a sparkle as she stared at Tulsi.

Her words affirmed what Tulsi had suspected. This food was meant to trip her up, but she wouldn't give Lucas's mother the satisfaction. "Actually, I'm neither. I was raised Catholic. We went to church every

Sunday, at least until I was in high school. We stopped going when my brother, Thomas, was on a traveling soccer team. I don't actually practice now that I'm an adult. I haven't had time to join a congregation since I moved here."

Mr. Campbell piped in, "You will someday. I find the older I get, the more religious I become."

Rather than comment, Tulsi nodded her understanding before continuing to eat. Not that she was surprised, but she found the food delicious. The mixture of textures, tastes, and spices enthralled her senses. Even the chicken gizzards. She was reluctant about eating it, but the thought of playing into Mrs. Campbell's hand made her try it. The taste surprised her. It was creamy and meaty. She actually liked it and ate it all with relish.

"Tell us about yourself, Tulsi," Mr. Campbell invited, after his wife had brought in cups of tea and coffee to serve with the flan she made for dessert.

"I was born in New Jersey. About the age of three, I was placed for adoption. I ended up with the Anthonys. I did my undergraduate degree at Rutgers before going to vet school at Cornell."

"So, you are a veterinarian," Mr. Campbell said. "Are you working here in Colby?"

"I am now. At the Colby County Veterinary Clinic. It's owned by my former vet school classmate. She invited me to come work here. And I'm loving it."

Before he could ask another question, Tulsi's phone rang. When she saw the caller ID, she set her coffee cup down and stood abruptly. "I'm sorry, I have to take this call."

She stepped into the hallway. "Hey, what's up?" As the overnight tech explained the situation, Tulsi listened intently. An in-house patient was acting restless, which could indicate problems. "Give her two milligrams of Gabapentin. I'll come in."

When she returned to the dining room, everyone looked at her expectantly.

She smiled. "A post-surgery patient is getting restless. Not something we like to see." She turned to Lucas and his parents, "My apologies, but I have to go back to the clinic." Tulsi turned to her host and hostess. "Everything was delicious. Truly. Thank you."

"Let me drive you," Lucas offered, standing and digging for keys in his jeans pocket.

"No, no, that's okay. I'll go by myself. It shouldn't take long." Relieved to finally have an excuse to skirt the inquisition, she grabbed her purse.

Lucas kissed her. "I'll wait up," he said as she left the house by the side door off the kitchen.

CHAPTER THIRTY-SEVEN

The cat finally settled after a couple of hours. As it was a post-op patient, Tulsi didn't want to overwhelm the feline's system any more than necessary. It was after midnight when she drove down Sparrow Street. Nearing the house, she saw two figures lurking on the front lawn. It looked suspicious as they carried what looked like buckets. Her breath accelerated. Something evil was going on. She could sense it in the tension in the figures as her car approached.

Memories of the house's damage on the night of the quinceañera sprang to mind. Fearing it was more mischief in progress, she pulled her car over two doors down from the Campbell home and got out. Whoever they were, they weren't just causing mischief; this was an act of malice. The two troublemakers stopped when they saw her, so she headed up the sidewalk to the door of the nearest mini mansion. When Tulsi reached the door, the vandals splashed the buckets' contents on the side of the Campbells' house.

She dialed 911 and reported the vandalism. Anger flared as the dispatcher asked far too many questions, and she hung up after giving them the street address and her name. Knowing she would need help, she called Lucas. Before he could say a word, she said, "Hey, someone's doing something to the front of your house!" She hung up. Adrenaline surging as she raced through the yards toward the culprits.

"Hey! Stop that," she yelled as loudly as possible. Chastising herself for calling the police first instead of stopping the vandals, she ran as hard as she could to stop them from doing more damage. The entire sprint, her mind questioned the wisdom of her actions.

Who the hell did she think she was to get involved? The Campbells wanted to keep their peaceful way of life here as much, if not more, than these neighbors did. The Campbells were living here first. What exactly did she intend to do that might make this situation better? Would apprehending the suspects make the neighborhood accept the

Campbells more? Probably not, but Tulsi couldn't think of it that way. These delinquents needed to be stopped. *No one* wants to have this happen to their home. Why couldn't these people understand that it had nothing to do with cultural differences and skin color? Her courage reared, spurring her on to stop the wrongdoing.

One kid turned, saw her coming, and flung some of the bucket's contents at her. She saw it coming and held her breath, hoping it wasn't acid or gasoline or something foul, caustic, or flammable. An involuntary shiver raced through her as the cold, viscous, paint-smelling material hit her head and chest, covering her in goo. She wiped her face, pushing away enough goo to see the boy running away. The other boy had frozen, watching his buddy drench her. Beyond furious, Tulsi growled as she ran toward him. He dropped the bucket on his feet and ran after the first guy. Tulsi picked up the bucket, hoping to stop the paint from leaking into the lawn.

Sirens became louder as police cruisers turned onto the street. The front porch light went on, and Mr. Campbell, Mrs. Campbell, and Lucas ran out onto the stoop.

Tulsi pointed in the direction the two boys had run as the policeman jumped out of the cruiser. Instead of running to apprehend them, he advanced on her and yelled, "Police. Drop your weapon. Put your hands up."

My weapon? Her mind reeled when she realized her predicament. She was holding the bucket, covered in paint. The same paint splashed on the front of the Campbells' house. Panic jolted through her chest. This wasn't how it was supposed to end. She was the good guy.

Another police officer arrived, his gun drawn, and focused on her. "Drop it and put your hands up." Sweating profusely, barely able to stand on her rubbery legs, she let the bucket drop and held her hands up over her head.

TULSI'S FLAME

As the police officer put handcuffs on her slender wrists, Mrs. Campbell approached, pointing a finger at Tulsi. "You! I knew it had to be you destroying our house. You little—"

Lucas stepped between his mother and Tulsi. "Mama, she caught the vandals red-handed and interrupted their plan. She called me and told me they were outside the house." He turned to the policeman, "Officer, I swear that's the truth."

Tulsi shivered, her knees feeling almost too weak to stand. The police officer's flashlight revealed she was drenched with bright fuchsia and yellow paint. Tulsi's gut roiled with anger. This had all gone wrong. She should have stayed out of it. Why did *she* have to stop the vandals? Why get in the fray? Why try to help Lucas's family as they dealt with the neighborhood's prejudice? The thought that Lucas's mother would accuse her of doing the damage had never entered her mind.

Tears rolled down her cheeks, but she couldn't wipe them away. When she turned her head to try to wipe her cheek on her shoulder, she noticed paint footprints on the grass. "Look at the footprints. Follow them. Both of them went that way." Unable to point, she jerked her head in the direction they led. Another officer turned his flashlight to the grass, illuminating the prints.

Mr. Campbell, Lucas, and the police officer followed the paint four houses down the street. The officer knocked on the door and was let inside.

Knowing the officer had the situation under control, Lucas returned to Tulsi. "The footprints led us to the house. Paint was smeared on the doorknob. It's pretty clear where the vandals went."

His mother turned on him. "Don't you protect this puta. She's behind it. The mastermind. Look how much paint she got on herself doing it."

Lucas's face contorted with rage, his hands fisted at his sides. He straightened up tall in front of his mother. "Don't you dare accuse Tulsi of doing this stupid shit. You've got it all wrong. She tried to stop those punks. You should be grateful Tulsi's actions managed to catch them."

Mrs. Campbell burst into tears. "Lucas, bebé, hear me out..." she cried.

Lucas put up his hands. "No. I don't want to hear it. I'm not a baby, and I can take care of myself. I learned my lesson the hard way with Sammy. Tulsi Anthony didn't have anything to do with this."

Mr. Campbell arrived and laid a hand on his wife's shoulder. "It's true, Carmen. The police have the vandals in custody. And the dispatcher verified that a woman named Tulsi Anthony called in the vandalism. Miss Anthony had nothing to do with it except to corner our culprits."

He turned to Tulsi as the officer removed the handcuffs. "Thank you, Tulsi. You have our gratitude." He looked her up and down. "Let's get you cleaned up."

CHAPTER THIRTY-EIGHT

"Hose me off out here," Tulsi said, standing on the grass beside the sidewalk to the front door. "I don't want to traipse paint all over your house."

"Mama, can you get a sheet? I want to wrap her in it when I'm done." His mother, with a sour look on her face, said nothing but strode into the house, her fist clenched at her sides.

At her suggestion, Lucas dragged the hose out from behind the shrubs and turned the nozzle on. While his father manned the flashlight, Lucas aimed it at her legs first.

"Holy crap!" Tulsi's teeth started chattering immediately. "It's so cold!"

"I'll take you inside for a hot shower, but I want to get as much paint off you as I can before we go inside." Lucas continued spraying her back. "Turn around so I can spray your front."

Shivering violently, she turned, her arms bent, covering her chest, trying to keep whatever warmth might remain in her torso.

"Drop your arms so I can get your chest. That's where most of the paint is."

"L-lu-cas-s-s! I-I'm freezing!"

"Just a little bit more to go, and I'll stop," Lucas said, slowing the spray and attacking the paint in her hair.

Unable to stand the freezing water drenching her entire body, she yelled, "L-lu-luc-cas! Th-th-that's en-en-nough."

He shut off the nozzle. Grabbing the sheet his mother had brought, he wrapped it around Tulsi like a swaddle. "Hang tight. Let's get you in the house with minimal dripping."

Mrs. and Mr. Campbell entered the house to ready the bathroom so Tulsi could shower off the remaining paint.

Tulsi tried to walk, but the sheet held her too tight. Still shivering, she lost her balance, and if it hadn't been for Lucas catching her, she would have fallen over.

"Hang on, I have an idea," Lucas said as he swept her up to carry her into the house.

"Just loosen the sheet so I can walk," Tulsi protested, but Lucas wasn't minding her.

He strode up the stairs with her in his arms and into the second-floor bathroom. "I'll help you undress," he said as he set her feet down on the bathroom floor. Lucas twirled her around, unwrapping the sheet from her body, still covered with paint-stained clothes.

"No, you won't," Mama Campbell said, her arms crossed over her chest.

"Mama, she can't do it herself. Look at her." He nodded toward Tulsi as she crouched, shivering violently in her wet garments. "She can barely stand up. She could slip in the shower. Hurt herself."

Mrs. Campbell stared at her son and then Tulsi, scowling. "I will stay with her and help her."

Tulsi tried to stand up straight, her fingers trembling as she reached for the hem of her scrub top.

"Lucas, out," his mother ordered.

The set of Lucas's jaw revealed his frustration. His worry for Tulsi and his mistrust of his mother were obvious.

"I'll be fine," Tulsi said through chattering teeth. "P-please let me get into the hot shower."

"I'll be outside the door if you need anything." Lucas's eyes riveted to hers as his jaw clenched tight.

"Get her some clothes," his mother ordered again. "Graham, hot tea, please."

The two men disappeared to follow orders, and Mrs. Campbell closed the bathroom door.

TULSI'S FLAME

The fabric clung stubbornly to Tulsi's sodden skin, and her hands cramped with the cold. Mrs. Campbel silently removed Tulsi's scrub top, throwing it in the sink. Their eyes met, and Tulsi could see the hardness in Lucas's mother's eyes, the set of her jaw, and the disapproving look on her face at the sight of Tulsi's black, lacy bra. Breaking eye contact, Tulsi reached for the waistband of her pants to pull them down.

Lucas's mother remained silent as she placed Tulsi's garments in a plastic trash bag. "I'll launder these for you."

"N-n-no need. You can throw them out."

In her bra and panties, Tulsi stepped into the shower stall. Hot water poured from the nozzle. "Aaaah," she said as the steam and water worked its magic. With her eyes closed, she couldn't see Mrs. Campbell on the other side of the translucent shower curtain. The woman remained silent as Tulsi stood there, turning under the spray like a chicken on a spit, trying to warm every inch of her body.

"There's shampoo and body wash on the shelf," Mrs. Campbell grunted. Her silhouette on the dry side of the curtain pointed to the small corner shelf behind Tulsi.

Tulsi reached for the shampoo first, sudsing her hair and rinsing until no more paint color ran down onto the shower floor. "Turn around please," she called out to Mrs. Campbell.

"Why?" the woman responded, suspicion in her voice.

"I want to remove my underwear to use the body wash," Tulsi explained, her teeth clacking and her body no longer shaking like Jello.

Mrs. Campbell did as she was asked while Tulsi removed her bra and panties and washed up.

A knock on the door drew both of their attention. "Mama, I have the clothes."

While Tulsi finished washing her skin free of residual paint, Mrs. Campbell took the clothes from Lucas.

Tulsi could hear him ask, "How's she doing?"

"Fine. Where's your father with the tea?" she demanded. "Go find out," she ordered before slamming the door shut.

Tulsi contemplated getting out of the shower but knew Mrs. Campbell was still on the other side of the steamed-up shower curtain. Not sure what to do, she finally said, "Is there a towel out there?"

"Yes, wait," Mrs. Campbell said. "I'll be back. The towels are in the linen closet." She disappeared outside the bathroom for only a moment. Returning, she said, "I have the towel for you. Let me know when you want it."

Tulsi gave herself the luxury of another hot rinse before shutting off the water.

"I'm ready," she said, raking her fingers through her hair to tease out any tangles. She reached her hand outside the shower curtain and Mrs. Campbell thrust a large fluffy towel into it. She wrapped it around her torso, leaving her hair to drip. "Thank you."

She flung back the curtain. Mrs. Campbell stood in front of the sink, staring into the mirror. Their eyes met in the reflection.

"Do you have a smaller towel for my wet hair?"

Mrs. Campbell left the bathroom, returning quickly and held out the towel.

"Thank you." She reached for it and draped it around her hair as best she could.

Their eyes met in the mirror again. If she wasn't mistaken, Mrs. Campbell's look had softened.

"You have lovely hair." Mrs. Campbell said. It wasn't a sneer or a scowl. Her comment sounded genuine.

Tulsi almost stopped breathing at the shock of her statement. "Umm, thank you."

When she started to breathe again, she said the first thing that came to mind. "It's dark, like yours."

The two women locked eyes in the bathroom mirror over the sink a third time.

TULSI'S FLAME

"There's detangling spray on the shelf. And a comb." Mrs. Campbell said, gesturing to the shelving beside the sink. "I'll leave you to get dressed. Your clothing is there." She pointed to the clothes on the commode lid.

Tulsi saw the small pile of clothes Lucas had brought. "Thank you for your help."

Mrs. Campbell grunted something unintelligible before leaving the bathroom.

Quickly, Tulsi pulled on her underwear, yoga pants, a tee shirt, socks and a robe. Cocooned in the thick pile of fabric and lingering heat from the shower, Tulsi sat on the toilet lid. Mrs. Campbell's rather kind offer to help warmed Tulsi's heart. Getting drenched in paint and handcuffed might have been the best thing to melt some of Mrs. Campbell's animosity toward her.

A light rapping on the door sounded. "Tuls? Ready to come down for hot tea?" Lucas asked.

"Yes," she said, gathering up her remaining energy to return to the kitchen.

Downstairs, Mr. Campbell handed her a teacup. "I put some sugar and milk in it. Is that okay?"

Tulsi gave him a smile. His calming warmth, plus the hot shower and the long night, had her eyelids drooping. "Perfect, thank you."

A plate of shortbread sat in the middle of the table, though Mrs. Campbell was nowhere in sight.

Lucas and his father sat at the table while Tulsi drank her tea quickly. "If you don't mind, I'm going to bed. It's been quite the day. Thank you for everything." She meant it. Despite everything that had gone down tonight, she was grateful for their help.

Mr. Campbell rose from the table, placing a hand on each of her shoulders. "We thank you. Without your help, we would not have found the culprits. I'm only sorry you suffered."

Tulsi nodded. "Yes, well. I'll be fine in the morning." She stood up.

Lucas stood up. "I'll go with you."

He helped her to her room, gathered her in his arms, and held her. Fatigue settled heavily on her.

"I'm so sorry about everything," she whispered, her head resting on his shoulder. "Now let me go so I can get some sleep. I still have to go to work in a few hours."

CHAPTER THIRTY-NINE

As tired as she was, Tulsi couldn't sleep. Her mind kept repeating the evening's drama. She thought of all the things she did wrong and what she could have done better. It was useless thinking. What happened had happened, and there was no way of changing any of it. Mrs. Campbell's comment about her hair repeated itself every time she closed her eyes. It was a compliment and an unexpected one, at that. It sounded genuine. Perhaps Lucas's mother was feeling a little remorseful about her reactions during the altercation? She tossed and turned in the soft bed, the sheet and coverlet pulled up tight to her chin, her socks still on. She lay awake for hours before she slammed her eyes open and got out of bed to go down to the kitchen. Another cup of warm tea might help.

She filled a mug with water by the rays of a night-light, and heated it in the microwave. Opening several cabinets before finding the tea, she grabbed the Earl Grey and plunked a bag into her hot water. She stirred a spoonful of sugar into it and sat in the quiet kitchen, sipping her tea with her eyes closed.

The overhead light turned on. Tulsi's eyes flew open in surprise before blinking rapidly against the harsh, bright light.

Mrs. Campbell stood in the doorway. "What are you doing down here?" Her tone was suspicious, and she didn't advance into the room.

"I couldn't sleep. Too much excitement." Tulsi held up her mug. "I thought another warm tea might help. Care to join me?" Tulsi hoped the woman said no. She didn't want to be on edge, tense, and anxious over what Mrs. Campbell might say or do.

"Huh," Mrs. Campbell said before entering the kitchen. She pulled a mug from the cabinet, filled it with water and microwaved it to steaming before sinking a tea bag in it. She stared out the window over the sink into the darkness. "Are you feeling better?"

Tulsi nodded, though Mrs. Campbell didn't see. "Yes. The excitement, though. I keep thinking how I should have reacted differently."

"Why? Did you not want to stop the vandals?"

"Oh, I did want to stop them. That was the whole point. I'm glad I succeeded, even if it made a mess of trouble."

Mrs. Campbell was silent for a few minutes as the women sipped from their mugs. Mrs. Campbell turned toward Tulsi. "You have a good job." It was more a statement than a question. Was Lucas's mother probing her for more information?

It dawned on Tulsi that Lucas's mother needed some assurance that she was not a gold digger like his previous girlfriend. Sensing it was an important matter for his family, she answered, "Yes. I'm financially self-sufficient. I have my own car, my own apartment, and I take care of myself. I don't need a man or anyone else to support me."

Tulsi could feel Mrs. Campbell's tension ease. "I—" She didn't know how to say what she was feeling, but she didn't want to miss the opportunity to set the record straight. She didn't think. She spoke her heart.

"Lucas and I, we're good together, we're friends. And our different cultures don't stand in the way of our love." Did she dare to say it? She took a big breath and steeled herself. "Just as your culture and Mr. Campbell's didn't stand in your way."

Mrs. Campbell turned around abruptly. Her face was tense again. But as the two women stared at each other, she sighed, and all tension ran from her face and body. "I can't deny that. We never expected to fall in love either. But here we are," she raised her palms, "forty-five years, five children, and nine grandchildren later." She flashed Tulsi a grimace before shrugging.

"How did you meet?" Tulsi asked.

For the first time, Mrs. Campbell smiled. "Ah. He was working for the airline on the island, inspecting local airports following Hurricane

David. I was helping to hand out food and water bottles. There wasn't any power, no lights, and transportation between the towns and cities on the island was impossible." Her smile broadened, lighting up her entire face. "I handed him a plate of food, and he said, 'Thank you' in that warm, thick Scottish brogue." She shook her head, still smiling. "I was instantly in love. I found out later he was too."

"That sounds amazing," Tulsi whispered. "I'm sure it wasn't easy, though."

"Easy? Not at all. Everywhere we turned, we were menaced. The racism, the inability for people to understand that your head can't tell your heart who to love...it so often wore us down, made us question our sanity and our feelings." She smiled broadly. "In the end, it only made us stronger as a couple."

"I believe that."

She sipped at her tea before adding, "I didn't want any of my children to undergo that kind of struggle. A struggle of love against the world. Times are better now. It's more acceptable. But there are still those who would discriminate against cross-cultural relationships. I prayed the Campbell bairns would not have to face that."

Tulsi took Mrs. Campbell's hand. "I understand. I wish it wasn't so difficult either. It's been so hard on Lucas to watch his family pull away because of me. And it breaks my heart to see him in such pain over it." She looked Mrs. Campbell in the eye as tears dripped down her cheeks. "If you can find it in your heart to let us be a couple, it would help us immensely."

Mrs. Campbell mashed her lips together, swiped a stray tear from her cheek, and rubbed her nose. She pulled Tulsi into a bear hug, and the two of them cried. After a few minutes, she pulled back. "You be good to my son."

Tulsi's heart lightened like a helium balloon. "I will always be good to Lucas."

Mrs. Campbell swiped at her cheeks again, wiping away her tears. "Bueno."

A firm knock on the door sounded and Mr. Campbell's worried voice boomed through the kitchen, "Is everything alright in there?"

"We are both fine." Mrs. Campbell answered.

CHAPTER FORTY

At lunchtime the next day, Tulsi made a phone call. "Kamal?"

"Yes! Tulsi. How are you?" Kamal asked.

"It's been a wild few days." She decided to cut out the niceties. "I've decided not to go with you. To India, I mean. I can't leave work right now, and frankly, it's too painful to immerse myself in the drama."

Kamal's end of the conversation was silent. At last, he sighed heavily. "I am disappointed but I do understand." He paused again before adding, "I want to answer your last question. The one I didn't get a chance to answer at your condo."

Tulsi's body tensed as she steeled herself. "Okay..."

"Nani said she couldn't handle both of us, and her financial resources were limited. She hoped, in time, the Patel family would want to support me. If they did, she'd try to get you back." He paused and sighed. "The Patels rebuffed her inquiries. It broke her heart when she learned the Anthonys adopted you so quickly. She knew getting you back would be almost impossible, even if she had the money to care for us both. She went to her grave wishing things had turned out as she hoped."

His confession left a lump in Tulsi's throat so big she couldn't reply.

"Can we stay in contact? You know, not every day or anything like that. I just want to know you are alive and doing okay," Kamal asked so quietly she almost didn't hear his voice.

Tulsi cleared her throat with a cough, and a hint of a smile rose on her face. "It is kind of nice knowing I have another brother. I think we can manage it." She changed the subject before she changed her mind. "So you're going to India alone?"

"No, didn't I tell you, my girlfriend is going with me...would have gone with you and me too."

"Learn something new about you every day," Tulsi muttered. "Great. I'm glad you have some emotional support. Call me when you get back. I'd like to hear how it all went."

"You got it, sister."

CHAPTER FORTY-ONE

A week later, Lucas called Dawson's cell phone. "Hey. I need some advice."

"What's up? Problems with the new post already?"

"Did you hear about it?" Hearing Dawson laugh, he said, "Ah, forget it. Look, I'm Puerto Rican and a new lieutenant at Station Three. What do you think is happening?" Lucas couldn't help the sarcasm in his voice. His gut was all tied up in knots from the disrespect he was receiving at Station Three. "They don't take me seriously, ignore my requests, and do things at their own pace. I can't make any headway. And Captain Walton is no help."

The issues started on Lucas's first shift. Captain Walton had introduced him to the firefighters on shift. "Let's welcome Lieutenant Campbell-Lopez to Station Three. He's replacing former Lieutenant Seeway, who is now Captain Seeway at Station Two. I know I don't have to remind you all to show our new officer the ropes here and give him his due." That said, the Captain returned to his office, leaving Lucas to stare at the six firefighters.

It was all downhill after that. No one offered to show him around the station. Since it was built later than Station Two, the layout and storage of equipment and supplies were different. When he asked firefighter Nolan to show him the station, Nolan rolled his eyes and walked away, taking refuge in the bathroom. Lucas's shoulders sank a little, but he straightened up, realizing the other five firefighters were watching him. "Anyone want to show me around?"

The answer to his question was delivered as the remaining five walked away toward the rec room. Lucas followed, expecting them to give him the rundown. Instead, all five flopped on the chairs and couch and stared at the television mounted to the far wall. One of them turned up the volume.

Realizing he was going to have to do it himself, he spent the next hour going through every room, every cabinet, and every nook and cranny in the building. All the while, he made notes on the locations of fire equipment and supplies. In a way, the time alone lifted his spirits. Without having to chit-chat with anyone, he could spend as much time as needed figuring out the logistics of the station. It eased his stomachache and gave him time to shake off the lack of welcome.

What didn't ease his nerves was the disarray in the storage rooms and apparatus. Both rigs were smeared with dust and mud. It looked like someone hadn't washed them in a few days. The engine and tanker's cabinets were disorganized. Cabinet labels didn't match the contents and the contents looked as though they were thrown in and the doors slammed shut. Nothing looked secure, not even the firehoses.

At Station Two, the team ensured that everything was in its place each morning, and the apparatus was washed, windows cleaned, and interior cabs vacuumed. Lucas made notes as he went along, a to-do list he'd jump on the guys to fix.

The rest of the day had been the same. Unlike Station Two, this outpost didn't have a cook. Everyone brought something from home, usually leftovers they warmed in the microwave. Lucas gave out assignments while the guys and Captain Walton ate in the kitchen. "Carlton, I'd like you to wash the tanker, including the windows inside and out, and vacuum the interior cabs. Kerman, I'd like you to do the same with the engine." Lucas pointed to two guys seated together. "Puglisi and Dyson, go through every compartment on the engine and make sure the equipment label on the door matches the material inside. Nolan and Hines, you're to do the same on the tanker." Only one guy appeared to be listening. "Report back when your assignments have been completed."

All six firefighters turned to Captain Walton, their eyes hard, not saying a word. Captain Walton picked up his lunch and strode off in the direction of his office, also without a word.

And Lucas knew he was fucked.

"So you're saying, you gave them direct orders and they never completed them?" Dawson asked, incredulity in his voice. "I knew those guys were assholes, but this is insubordination."

"Do you think it's because I'm new or because of my skin tone?"

"It doesn't matter. Report each of them to headquarters for insubordination. After what happened with Korth, the deputy chief and chief aren't going to want another episode of maleficence."

"Do you think so? Korth was a one-off problem."

Dawson sighed. "The upper echelon has been wanting to straighten out Station Three for a long time. The Korth incident made them all look bad because, despite all the documentation I had about him, they failed to do anything. So you need to document everything and get management behind you."

"But I'm not talking about one person. It's everyone. They can't shut down an entire station."

"Don't forget there are two other sets of firefighters at Station Three. They rotate. If the deputy chief orders the B or C shift to cover the station, you can bet your ass your guys are going to catch some flak from them. Peer pressure and management threats of severance will win the day for you."

"I don't know, Dawson." If Lucas's gut was tight before, it was now as twisted as a bowline knot. "This isn't what I expected."

"Have you noticed there are only white men on that shift? No women, no Blacks, no foreign-born firefighters of any kind. Don't you let them get away with it. I believe the selection committee picked you to help them bring that station up to par."

"You think so?" Lucas asked. The potential vote of confidence from his higher-ups, minus Captain Walton, eased some of his tension.

"I know so, Lucas. Don't worry. Stand your ground. Don't drop the hose line and run."

"Okay. I'll go into the main office tomorrow and fill out reports."

CHAPTER FORTY-TWO

The Colby County Fair started at nine o'clock Saturday morning. Tulsi, Alissa, and Alissa's sister had to be there by seven to set up the booth. The three women struggled to get the canopy up. They might have ditched it back in Tulsi's SUV if they weren't expecting it to be so sunny and hot that day. Luckily, Colby Animal Control had their own booth beside theirs. It made perfect sense with Animal Control's adoption facility in their booth. Not only would Tulsi answer questions at the booth table, but she also could monitor the status of the animals up for adoption during the event. Andrew and Gordon helped put up the clinic's canopy after finishing their set up.

As she waited for the start of the event, Tulsi paced the confines of the booth, cracking her knuckles, a worried look on her face.

"Settle down, Doc. We have nine hours of this. Might as well get off your feet while you can," Alissa said from her folding chair behind a side table. Beside Alissa sat her sister, Monique. "Can we move this jar to the front table?" Alissa wrinkled her nose. "It's pretty gross looking. I don't want to look at it all day."

"Yeah, pretty disgusting. It might bring more people to our booth if you put it on the front table," Monique added. "Where'd you get it?"

The jar held a dog's heart filled with heartworm. It was meant to drive the message that it was a serious infection and canine owners should be giving their dogs heartworm medication each month. "The local veterinary pathology lab provided the jar with the heart. They use it for show and tell at events, too. They let me borrow it for today." Tulsi moved the jar to her table.

Her stomach was upset but not from the jar's contents. This was not her element. If she could have gotten out of this chore, she would have. She ground her teeth. It made the most sense for her to be here instead of Hannah, who was still experiencing morning sickness.

Hannah was better off at the clinic handling any emergencies that arrived, and close to a bathroom should the need arise.

One of the organizing members came by. "Just wanted to make sure you have everything you need."

Tulsi stopped pacing. "How about a map of the festival set up? Where's the food, and where's the fire department booth?"

The woman fumbled with her clipboard, finally extracting a map of the grounds. "Here's the latest map." She pointed at it. "This here's the main food area though there's a few concession stands set up all around." She pointed to another area of the map. "Here's the Colby Fire Department booth, right here with some other town departments."

Tulsi made a mental note of these areas before the woman walked off to the Animal Control booth. Lucas was supposed to be covering the nine to noon shift at the fire department booth. Maybe she could run over to see him during a lull in the crowd traffic if it wasn't too far.

There wasn't a lull. On such a bright sunny day, it seemed everyone came to the festival, swamping the wide twelve-foot aisles. Tulsi, Alissa, and Monique were busy all day, answering questions, talking about the clinic's services, and setting up appointments for new clients. Tulsi was the busiest, answering questions about diseases, care, and health issues. Leo, tucked safely in his cage, and the jar drew the fascination of the crowds, especially the children. Tulsi didn't have any trouble answering the children's questions. Learning about animals and their care would potentially make them more compassionate to animals.

Just after noon, Mayor Analis stopped at the booth. "Doctor Anthony, it's a pleasure to meet you. Welcome to Colby."

Tulsi shook the mayor's proffered hand. "It's a lovely town. I'm looking forward to learning more about it over time."

"Good." The mayor stepped closer to Tulsi. "I wanted to ask you about possibly serving on a town committee I'm trying to put together. We've had some problems with people. Especially those who are reluctant or outright hostile to our blossoming immigrant population.

I'm wondering if you might be interested in a seat on this volunteer committee?"

The mayor's question shot a burst of energy through Tulsi. "Me?"

"Sure. Why not? I think you would be terrific lending your experiences to help some townspeople become more accepting of those from different cultures, ethnicities, and religious affiliations. Will you think about it and let me know?"

Tulsi nodded as her thoughts returned to the vandalism and animosity the Campbell family had experienced in their neighborhood. If she could help the community become more open and accepting, it would help the Campbells and so many others like them. "I'll get back to you soon."

Hands wrapped around Tulsi from behind, covering her eyes. "Guess who?"

She giggled, pulling Lucas's hands away and turning around to hug him. In his dress uniform, he looked so handsome, Tulsi's mouth watered, and her insides fluttered. "I'm so glad you stopped over. How's it going in your booth?"

"Fine. The kids are getting a kick out of climbing on the fire truck and sitting in the driver's seat." His smile warmed parts of Tulsi's body despite the inconvenient location. "And we put out some fire gear too; boots, bunker pants, a helmet, and a turnout coat."

"Sounds like fun. I'll try to stop over."

"My new truck arrives on Tuesday. So they tell me." Lucas's eyes sparkled, and his face beamed.

"That's great, sweetheart! Will you give me a ride in it?" Tulsi wiggled her eyebrows and gave him what she hoped was a seductive look.

A grin spread across his face, ear to ear. "I'll give you a ride, all right." He stared at her with lust in his eyes.

Tulsi licked her lips.

Lucas blinked and nodded before glancing at his watch. "Oops."

She glanced at her watch. "Oh, it's ten after twelve. Are you leaving now?"

"I am. I have to go home. The paint company is repainting my parents' house today. I'll see you later, right?"

"I'll be exhausted, but yes, I'll be home by about eight. I might stop by the clinic to make sure everything's okay."

"Give me a call when you're home." Lucas gave her another hug, topped with a passionate kiss that had Tulsi's toes curling, and left.

As he walked away, Tulsi overheard Alissa speaking to a couple.

"Dr. Anthony is new to our clinic and is a terrific veterinarian. She's a reptile, amphibian, and exotics specialist." Alissa beamed proudly and gestured toward Tulsi. "She's right here if you have any questions."

Tulsi's heart thudded in her chest. She had never heard any of the clinic staff lavish *any* praise on her. She blinked rapidly to keep the stinging tears at bay. With a broad smile, she joined the couple standing in front of Leo's tank.

"Hi, we were wondering if you ever hold any group trainings for the care of reptiles?" The man looked at the woman, and together they nodded.

"The clinic has been talking about having a reptile, amphibian, and exotic creature support group. Is that something you would be interested in?"

Their faces brightened. "Oh, yes. We have a rather informal group of people who meet at the local diner once a month to discuss our questions and concerns," the woman explained.

The man added, "We could easily let everyone know if you can provide us with information about when it will start."

"Sure thing," Tulsi said, picking up her business card from the table. "Give me a call in a week or so, and I'll see what I can pull together."

"We'll do that." The couple took the card and walked away, excitedly chattering about the prospects of a real group.

The rest of Tulsi's afternoon flew by quickly. Her knees had stopped shaking a while ago, and the surge of warmth in her chest left her feeling buoyant and happy. Talking with strangers was a lot easier when you knew what you were talking about. In the back of her mind, she already knew she would say yes to the mayor's proposal. The support group, she knew, Hannah would love. They had only talked about it once, but Hannah knew how much it meant to Tulsi to help people with their special critters.

As she drove to the clinic that evening, she couldn't wait to tell Hannah and Lucas all about the two opportunities. They left a warm feeling in her heart as she realized both were opportunities to join the Colby community on a new level. A level that accepted her as she was, as her training, education, and experience fostered. Excitement made goosebumps erupt on her arms. She was welcomed here, in this town, and it made her soul sing.

CHAPTER FORTY-THREE

Later that evening, Tulsi changed into yoga pants and a tee shirt before calling Lucas. "Hey, I'm home."

"How did the remainder of your day go?" he asked. "Want me to come over?" The hopeful tone in his voice sounded only halfhearted. It was his day off from the firehouse, and she knew he was on shift the next morning at seven a.m.

"Yes, but nah, stay home and rest." Feeling smug, she told Lucas about the discussion with the couple about the support group. "I'm going to push Hannah to let me do it, even if it's only on my evening off."

Lucas chuckled. "That's great, sweetie. I can hear how happy that makes you."

"It does. I'm looking forward to doing it." She yawned into the phone. "Sorry, my eyelids are barely open."

"I get it. I'm not long for the world of the awake either." He was silent a moment before adding, "Tulsi?"

She yawned again. "Sorry—"

"Tulsi, I want you to know, I love you." Lucas sounded calm and serious. "I—" He paused and started again. "You and me. We're a great team. I know we're both busy with our careers, but I want you to know, I see us together in the future. You and me."

Tulsi's breath caught in her chest. "A future?"

"Yup. I hope you're as serious about me as I am about you."

A tingle ran up her spine at his words. "Of course I am. I would like nothing better than to spend as much time with you as possible."

"Good. Because I'm searching for a house and want you to help me select one. Something you'd consider making your home in. Someplace where we could grow old together."

Tears filled her eyes. It was a near proposal. Lucas loved her and wanted to grow old with her.

Lucas said, "'Grow old along with me, Tulsi. The best is yet to be.'"

The flow of tears down her cheeks increased. "Robert Browning," she whispered.

"Yes," Lucas whispered back. "Do you think you might like to do that?"

"Aye." Tulsi sighed over the warmth ignited in her body. "Lucas, I changed my mind. Get over here."

His voice was soft, mellow, and, if she wasn't mistaken, full of love. "I'll be right there."

CHAPTER FORTY-FOUR

"Thanks for zooming again," Tulsi said to Hannah and Cortland.

Cortland replied, "Actually, I was going to call you guys. You'll never guess what happened." The lightness in her voice indicated it was something good for a change. She didn't wait for them to guess. "Dawson is here. He showed up on my doorstep a couple nights ago."

Hannah looked stunned. "I thought he was going to Ohio?"

"So did I," Tulsi confirmed. Why hadn't Lucas told her about this change in Dawson's plans? "Like to stay?"

"Yes! Can you believe it?" Cortland gushed. "He's got a deputy chief's job in Whittier, Alaska, about an hour away. So he's bunking in with me."

"Congrats, girlfriend. That's great news," Hannah said.

"Well, I have some news too. Lucas's mother and family have decided to accept me. It's such a relief to me and to Lucas. What a load of stress totally relieved. And...drumroll please, he got the promotion to lieutenant. He's ordered his new truck, bright red again." Tulsi rolled her eyes, and her two friends laughed. "He's doing well after a rough start in the new position. Some of the guys gave him a lot of grief, but the main office put five guys on unpaid leave for a week for insubordination. The sixth was fired outright because of a previous insubordination charge."

Hannah asked, "How's it going now? Did everyone straighten up and play right?"

"They did. It's been going well since. The guys were required to apologize to him, too. Lucas made a lot of brownie points with the deputy chief for rectifying the slovenly situation and straightening out the station. Which means, we're going to be buying a house together here in Colby."

"Together? As in living in sin?" Cortland chuckled.

Tulsi dropped the bomb, "As in, we're talking about marriage!"

Hannah and Cortland congratulated her. "Where's the ring?" Hannah asked, flashing her own ring finger where a new band of gold and Andrew's grandmother's engagement ring sat side by side.

"Nothing's official yet. We're just talking," Tulsi reiterated.

Hannah said, "Tulsi, tell Cortland about the festival."

Tulsi's face flushed hot. "I manned the booth at the Colby Festival. I have to say it wasn't bad. In fact, I met some really nice people and helped a few with their pets." It was true; she had felt a welcoming connection with the people who stopped at the booth. Between the mayor asking her to be part of a new town committee and the exotics support group, she would be an active member of her community. "I'm on the newly formed committee for the town." She couldn't help but smile. It felt like a win-win for her. By helping to make Colby a more inclusive place, she felt respected and accepted as a member of the community. And, she had to note, it warmed her soul. "And I'm hoping to help the Sparrow Street community come together to understand the Campbell-Lopez family. It's another win-win for Lucas and me, and his folks."

"That's so great, Tulsi. I'm so glad you're feeling welcome in Colby. It's a great little town." Cortland's visage turned as if to look at Hannah. "What's with the two last names?"

Tulsi remembered asking Lucas that question. "His father's last name is Campbell, and his mother's maiden name is Lopez, which she kept as her last name informally. Her official married name is Campbell. However, in Puerto Rico and other Spanish countries, the children inherit the mother's last name, with the father's surname name before the mother's. Here, officially, he's Campbell as well, but in respect to his culture, he hyphenates it informally."

Both Cortland and Hannah looked confused. "So what do we call him? Campbell or Lopez, or Campbell-Lopez?"

Tulsi laughed, "He'll answer to any of the above."

"Sorry I asked." Cortland rolled her eyes. "What about you, Hannah? Any good news to share? Know the sex of the baby yet?"

"Besides starting to feel like I've swallowed a beach ball? I told the clinic staff about my impending maternity leave. Everyone had already figured it out." Hannah smiled. "And Andrew and I decided to forgo a gender reveal. We want to be surprised."

"How could they not know when you were running to the bathroom to throw up all the time?" Tulsi laughed. "I'm surprised Frances didn't pick up on it."

"Speaking of Frances, Cortland, we've had some great candidates applying for Frances's job. Tulsi and I hope to make our selection this week after the final candidate's interview."

Cortland sniffled. "I wish I could be there. Don't forget to invite me to any baby showers, Tulsi. I'll make the trip."

Tulsi nodded, "You got it."

"You know, I miss our old vet school days. But despite the miles, I think we've become even closer. Each of us found our happily ever after. Each of us found a love we deserved, too." She paused, "what more could we ask for?"

Acknowledgements:

Thank you to my BFF, Judy, for the break I needed when my writing spirit was low. Your friendship, and our fun together exploring the Northern New York area cleared my mind and helped to see this novel to completion. Thank you, my dear friend, for all your love and support of my writing endeavors. Knowing you and being your friend is a privilege.

To Karen Fine, author of "The Other Family Doctor". A wonderful, heartfelt book by a veterinarian, that gave me a glimpse into what it means to be a vet in these times.

To my CTRWA critique group (AK, Grace, Connie, Ryan, Shayne, Gail, Carole, Krista, et.al.) for reading my sucky WIP (work in progress) and kindly opening my eyes to all its flaws.

Thanks to Kristen G. for all her suggestions of Puerto Rican foods.

A special shout out to Connie Jagodzinski, author of "Maid of Honor" among other books, for her suggestions on the reconciliation scene.

My editor, Lynne Hancock Pearson... I'm amazed you still want to work with me! I am so grateful for all your editorial hard work, comments and criticisms that help reshape my manuscript into something worth publishing. A special thank you for suggesting, "Relatable Writing, A Writers for Diversity Workbook" by Eliana West. I highly recommend it to any writer with a diverse cast of characters.

FIRST CHRISTMAS ORNAMENT

Chapter One

"Special order, a Rueben with a fried egg," Vanessa said, setting the order slip on the countertop before disappearing through the kitchen door at Jam Bakery.

"Oh, that sounds yum," Isabelle Becker said aloud as she started making the breakfast sandwich. The fresh, free-range egg sizzled on the small hot griddle in the corner kitchen space. Behind her, the morning baking crew was finishing up preparing the bread and pastries for the day. She threw the corned beef on the griddle for a few seconds to warm it up and dropped the Swiss cheese on top, giving it a half minute to melt. The aromas made her mouth water as she assembled the stack of fried egg, corned beef, cheese, sauerkraut, and Russian dressing to the lightly toasted rye bread. Thinking she had to make one for herself tomorrow morning, she wrapped the breakfast sandwich in foil before dropping it in a paper bag.

Snatching the order slip up from the countertop, she glanced at the name. "Gilbert." She smiled as a wave of reminiscence spread through her chest. She had loved that name since first seeing the *Anne of Green Gables* miniseries as a little girl decades ago. The character, Gilbert Blythe, eventually became Anne Shirley's husband. The actor who played him soared to instant fame with teenage females for his good looks and dreamy countenance. Isabelle remembered taping his picture all over her school locker. Her mind wandered further as she threw a handful of napkins into the paper bag. Gilbert was also the name of a friend of hers in high school. *What ever happened to Gilbert Darrow?* He was also kind of dreamy looking, but they had only been friends; fellow classmates and the rest of their clique hung out between classes, during lunch, and study halls.

The swinging doors bounced open as she walked from the kitchen into the front sales and dining area. Not looking at the small crowd at the counter, she held up the bag and yelled, "Gilbert."

A man stepped forward. "Isabelle?"

Startled, she looked at the customer, her arm dropping to her side, the bag still in hand. "Gil? Gil Darrow?" And here he was, in the flesh, and boy oh boy did that flesh look mighty fine. The last time she had seen him, Gil still looked like a scrawny teenager. Here he was filled out into mouth-watering manhood.

"I thought you were in Chicago." His sparkling blue eyes peered out from under an errant wave of red-brown hair.

His sawdust-laced jeans, chambray shirt, and a two or three-day-old scruff gave him a down-home, country look that made her mouth go dry. She cleared her throat to get it working again. "Uhm, I was in Chicago for college. I've been back in Vermont for a while now."

"Hmm." His gaze roamed over her face before dropping to her hand.

"Oops, sorry. Here you go. I hope you enjoy it." She held out the paper bag. "It's great to see you again." When he took it from her, her eyes lingered on his body a moment before she turned and headed for the kitchen door.

"Isabelle, wait," he called out.

She froze in her tracks, her heart thumping faster at the sound of his voice.

When she turned back, he added, "Can you join me for a few minutes?"

"Let me see if they have any more work for me." She eyed the two workers at the counter. "Jenny, any more sandwich orders?" When Jenny shook her head as she made change for a customer, Isabelle turned back. "Yes, for a few minutes."

The two old friends walked across the black and white checked tile floor to an unoccupied café table in the back of the room. "Mind if I eat?" Gilbert asked before sipping his coffee.

"Of course not. Eat it while it's hot." Isabelle didn't know what to do with her hands, folding them in her lap at first, then across her chest. Not wanting to appear closed to conversation by body language, she changed them again, clasping them together and resting them on the tabletop.

Gilbert tore into the bag, took a bite of his sandwich, rolled his eyes, and chewed, groaning his pleasure. "So good. Did you make it?"

Isabelle smiled. "I did." The last time she saw Gil was the night before he left to visit his grandparents in Arizona, just a month after high school graduation. The six years since then yawned wide between them, creating a chasm Isabelle didn't know how to bridge. Finally, her brain caught on one topic. "What are you doing here in Fulton River?"

ALSO BY DIANA ROCK

Fulton River Falls Series
Melt My Heart
Proof Of Love
Bloomin' In Love
First Christmas Ornament
Quest For Love

Colby County Veterinary Series
Bid To Love
Courting Choices
Tulsi's Flame

Standalone Novels
Hollywood Hotshot
Little Bit of Wait
Havilland's Highland Destiny

• • • •

DianaRock.com

Don't miss out!

Visit the website below and you can sign up to receive emails whenever Diana Rock publishes a new book. There's no charge and no obligation.

https://books2read.com/r/B-A-YUKN-GRXYC

BOOKS2READ

Connecting independent readers to independent writers.

About the Author

Diana lives in eastern Connecticut with her tall, dark and handsome hero and two mischievous felines. Diana likes puttering about the yard, baking and cooking, hiking, fly-fishing, and Scottish Country Dancing. Sign up for Diana's newsletter at DianaRock.com to receive special news, and free bonus material.

Read more at DianaRock.com.

Milton Keynes UK
Ingram Content Group UK Ltd.
UKHW031115261124
451585UK00004B/510

Tulsi's Flame
Colby County Veterinary Series, Volume 3
Diana Rock